Great American Writers

TWENTIETH CENTURY

EDITOR

R. BAIRD SHUMAN

University of Illinois

J. D. Salinger • Carl Sandburg

Jack Schaefer • Anne Sexton • Upton Sinclair

Isaac Bashevis Singer • Gertrude Stein

MARSHALL CAVENDISH

NEW YORK • TORONTO • LONDON • SYDNEY

Marshall Cavendish
99 White Plains Road
Tarrytown, New York 10591-9001

Website: www.marshallcavendish.com

© 2002 Marshall Cavendish Corporation

Library of Congress Cataloging-in-Publication Data

Great American writers: twentieth century / R. Baird Shuman, editor.
    v. cm.
    Includes bibliographical references and indexes.
    Contents: v. 1. Agee-Bellow--v. 2. Benét-Cather--v. 3. Cormier-
Dylan--v. 4. Eliot-Frost--v. 5. Gaines-Hinton--v. 6. Hughes-Lewis--v. 7.
London-McNickle--v. 8. Miller-O'Connor--v. 9. O'Neill-Rich--v. 10.
Salinger-Stein--v. 11. Steinbeck-Walker--v. 12. Welty-Zindel--v. 13.
Index.
    ISBN 0-7614-7240-1 (set)—ISBN 0-7614-7250-9 (v. 10)
    1. American literature--20th century--Bio-bibliography--
Dictionaries. 2. Authors, American--20th century--Biography--
Dictionaries. 3. American literature--20th century--Dictionaries. I.
Shuman, R. Baird (Robert Baird), 1929-

PS221.G74 2002
810.9'005'03
[B]   2001028461

Printed in Malaysia; bound in the United States

07 06 05 04 03 02   6 5 4 3 2 1

Contents

J. D. Salinger

BORN: January 1, 1919, New York, New York

IDENTIFICATION: Post-World War II novelist and short-story writer noted for capturing the voice of the postwar generation's youth and for disappearing from public view after the 1960s.

During the 1950s and 1960s, J. D. Salinger embodied the style of fiction writing that captured the voice of a generation unsure of itself and its place in the world following World War II. With a very small body of work—one true novel and a handful of short stories—he captured the pains of adolescence and the hearts of a legion of faithful readers. As his popularity increased, his growing frustration with the intrusiveness of public life led him to shun interviews and eventually publicity altogether. Salinger did, however, reappear into public view to defend his privacy and the legal rights of his works.

The Writer's Life

Jerome David Salinger was born January 1, 1919, in New York City, the son of a well-to-do Jewish cheese importer and a Scotch Irish mother. He grew up in the more fashionable neighborhoods of Manhattan and attended several public schools before enrolling in Valley Forge Military Academy in 1934. While at Valley Forge he began writing fiction, often at night underneath his covers with a flashlight. Among other things, he wrote the words to the school's anthem, which is still sung at graduation ceremonies. He graduated from Valley Forge in June 1936.

One of Valley Forge Military Academy's most distinguished sons, Salinger's own boarding school experience was refined and distilled into the tortured machinations of his literary alter ego Holden Caulfield, the protagonist of *The Catcher in the Rye*.

Education. For a brief time in 1937 Salinger enrolled at New York University, but he dropped out to pursue a brief career as an entertainer aboard the Swedish cruise liner *M. S. Kungsholm*. Later that year he went to Austria and Poland to learn more about the cheese business and to improve his skills in French and German. He returned home in 1938 and enrolled in Ursinus College in Collegeville, Pennsylvania. He continued to write, and he contributed to the school's newspaper but dropped out after only one semester. Salinger hated the rigors of academia and was not interested in college but told friends that someday he would write the "great American novel" and become famous.

In 1939 Salinger decided to give college another try and enrolled at Columbia University. There he participated in a short-story writing class taught by Whit Burnett, a highly influential writer and editor who founded *Story* magazine. The class made a large impact on Salinger, and in the spring of 1940 he published his first short story, "The Young Folks," in Burnett's magazine. Salinger was so enthused by his publication that he continued writing at full force. After a year of constant effort, he eventually broke into well-paying literary magazines such as the *Saturday Evening Post*, *Esquire*, *Mademoiselle*, and *Cosmopolitan*.

Europe. In December of 1941 the United States entered World War II. Salinger joined the army and was eventually shipped overseas in 1944. He participated in the attack on Normandy and served in the Counter Intelligence Corps in England. He later used his Counter Intelligence

Corps training ground of Devonshire, England, as a setting for the short story "For Esmé—with Love and Squalor." His experience uncovering members of the Gestapo would also become part of this story.

During this time Salinger continued to write, often carrying a typewriter with him in his jeep as he traveled. *Collier's* published his "Personal Notes of an Infantryman," an account of some of his war experiences. He also wrote "This Sandwich Has No Mayonnaise," which was published in the *Saturday Evening Post.* Salinger was beginning to become more aware of his literary voice and purpose.

On June 22, 1944, a relief platoon of American soldiers disembarks from a Coast Guard landing craft on the shores of Normandy. The war years filled the budding writer with a wealth of stark images.

Early Success. Salinger returned to New York after the war and continued writing. Some of the stories he wrote at this time, such as "Slight Rebellion off Madison," and "I'm Crazy," feature the first appearances of character Holden Caulfield. Between 1946 and 1951 Salinger began practicing what became known as the "*New Yorker* school of fiction," which represented a style of fiction that appealed to the young, sophisticated, and largely upper-class children of the parents that had survived both the Great Depression and World War II. Salinger also continued selling stories. One, "Uncle Wiggly in Connecticut," was bought by Hollywood producers and made into the film *My Foolish Heart* (1949), starring Susan Hayward and Dana Andrews. However, Salinger was so disappointed by the motion picture that he never again allowed any of his writing to be adapted for film.

In 1951 Salinger's groundbreaking novel, *The Catcher in the Rye,* was published. While some critics were slow to embrace it, the novel was adored by the reading public, especially those who were part of the incipient counterculture of the 1950s. Most enraptured of the novel were those who felt they closely resembled Holden Caulfield, the sixteen-year-old protagonist, who wishes to protect childhood innocence from the pain and hypocrisy of the world. Holden's narrative of a lonely and harrowing weekend in New York City after being expelled from school, told while in a psychiatrist's office, resonated with readers, and Salinger became an instant celebrity.

Two years later, Salinger released *Nine Stories,* which collected some of his stories from *The New Yorker* and contained the first stories of what would become the focus of Salinger's later fiction, the Glass family. The Glass family stories told episodes in the lives of seven gifted children of a retired vaudeville couple: Seymour, Buddy, Boo Boo, Walter, Waker, Zooey, and Franny. The collection contains one of Salinger's most famous stories, "A Perfect Day for Bananafish," and one of his most finely crafted stories, "For Esmé—with Love and Squalor."

Retreat to the Country. In January of 1953 Salinger left New York and moved to Cornish, New Hampshire, retreating to a cottage overlooking the Connecticut River. He was becoming increasingly tired of publicity and simply wanted to be left alone to write and study Eastern philosophy. When a local girl whom he

In the 1950s the increased interest in psychoanalysis and in the clinical session, suggested here by Diana Ong's painting *Group*, attracted many writers who wished to chart these unexplored mental landscapes. Their work assumed what some critics identified as a confessional dimension.

had befriended tricked him into an interview and then sold the interview to another paper, Salinger was so offended that he never again offered to be interviewed.

The year 1961 brought the publication of two more novellas in the Glass series of stories, published in one volume as *Franny and Zooey*. The last collection that Salinger would publish appeared in 1963 as *Raise High the Roof Beam, Carpenters, and Seymour: An Introduction*. He published only one more story, "Hapworth 16, 1924," which appeared in *The New Yorker* on June 19, 1965. The story takes the form of a long letter that Buddy Glass finds from his brother Seymour forty years after Seymour wrote it from summer camp at the age of seven. In 1967 Salinger ended his twelve-year marriage to Claire Douglas, whom he had married in 1955, and with whom he had two children, Margaret and Matthew.

The Private Author. From that moment, Salinger disappeared from public life, only reemerging from time to time to demand his privacy. In 1971 he took legal action against a man who was planning to publish some of Salinger's earlier stories without his authorization. In 1986 he filed suit to prevent author Ian Hamilton from publishing a biography of him that contained private letters he had written. Hamilton was forced to remove the letters, and in 1988 the book appeared as *In Search of J. D. Salinger*, an account of Hamilton's attempts to publish his book about Salinger.

Salinger said that he continued to write, if only for himself, and that he did not rule out the idea of publishing. Books about him continued to be published, including *At Home in the World* (1998), a memoir by Joyce Maynard, which tells of a relationship she had with Salinger in 1972 when she was eighteen and he was in his fifties.

The Writer's Work

J. D. Salinger's fiction tends to fall into two main categories: his novel, *The Catcher in the Rye*, which deals with Holden Caulfield, and his series of stories concerning the Glass family. All his fiction shares in common the style of language for which Salinger became famous, shaped by a rough and brusque tone that seemed to capture the confusion and pessimism of the post–World War II generation.

Manhattan. Salinger's fiction takes place in the boom years following the end of World War II, when the American economy was strong and prosperity seemed possible for everyone. The days of the Great Depression of the 1930s were far in the past, and New York City was at the height of its glory. Salinger was familiar with this world, and so, too, were his characters.

Holden Caulfield often refers to New York City's night life and its museums and fancy restaurants. The Glass children, former stars of a radio quiz show, "It's A Wise Child," are part of a modern and unconventional world much different from that of their elders, both in terms of their education and their beliefs. This unconventionality is shared by all of Salinger's characters and is often the source of their problems.

Postwar Manhattan, seen here in Xavier J. Barile's 1953 oil painting *42nd Street Nocturne* (Smithsonian American Art Museum, Washington, D.C.), was a bustling cultural and social mecca. It proved the perfect backdrop for Salinger's quirky and independent-minded characters, often too smart for their own good.

HIGHLIGHTS IN SALINGER'S LIFE

1919	J. D. Salinger is born in New York, New York.
1936	Graduates from Valley Forge Military Academy.
1936–1938	Travels overseas and attends several universities.
1939	Attends Columbia University and meets Whit Burnett.
1940	Publishes first short story, "The Young Folks," in Burnett's magazine *Story*.
1942–1944	Serves overseas in the U.S. Signal Corps and the Counter Intelligence Corps.
1946	Publishes story "Slight Rebellion off Madison" in *The New Yorker*.
1946–1951	Publishes seven stories in *The New Yorker*, including "A Perfect Day for Bananafish."
1951	Publishes *The Catcher in the Rye*.
1953	Moves to Cornish, New Hampshire, increasingly frustrated by publicity; publishes *Nine Stories*.
1955	Marries Claire Douglas, with whom he will have two children.
1961	Publishes *Franny and Zooey*.
1963	Publishes *Raise High the Roof Beam, Carpenters, and Seymour: An Introduction*.
1965	Runs last published story, "Hapworth 16, 1924," in *The New Yorker*.
1967	Is divorced from Claire Douglas.
1971	Files suit to prevent circulation of an unauthorized collection of his early short stories in California.
1986	Files suit to stop publication of Ian Hamilton's biography.
1987	Publication of biography by Hamilton is blocked.
1988	Hamilton publishes book as *In Search of J. D. Salinger*.
1998	Joyce Maynard publishes *At Home in the World*.
1999	Paul Alexander publishes *Salinger: A Biography*.

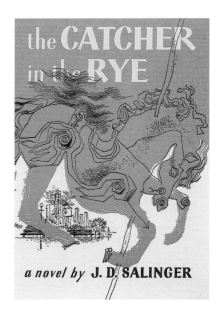

Themes of Isolation. Salinger's characters are often outsiders in society and do not know how to cope with this fact. Often this isolation is literal, as when Buddy Glass hides away in his dormitory in upstate New York, but more commonly it is an isolation that cannot be described physically. Holden Caulfield's loneliness stems from his desire to find some ideal place or person that may not even exist. He is unable to relate to his classmates and to everyone else, including his brother, D. B., whom he bundles together in the world of "phonies," and he finds himself lost in a world in which he does not fit.

Much of Salinger's personal life has been compared to that of Holden Caulfield's. Like his protagonist, Salinger changed schools several times and often did things that were considered unconventional and would get him expelled. Salinger also liked to embellish his own life story and would spin whatever yarn seemed fitting at the time, such as saying he was a goalie for a Montreal hockey team or that the Marx brothers had often visited his house when he was a child.

Characters' Realism. Salinger's characters are realistic both in their dialogue and in their

The Glasses are an unconventional, deeply symbiotic family, interdependent and united against the outside world, which does not fully understand or appreciate them. At the same time, like the figures that populate Gonzalo Cienfuegos's *Landscape with Characters and a Boy in Red*, their uniqueness is divisive and they stand alone, unable to truly communicate.

reactions to their situations. While *The Catcher in the Rye* may be remembered for its profanity, the most distinguishing thing about the language in the novel is how realistically close to common speech it is. Instead of speaking in flowery, stuffy prose, Salinger's characters swear, complain, mutter, worry, and deliver every other manner of speech in a realistic style. Because Holden Caulfield and Salinger's other characters speak in a natural manner, they become more vivid and realistic characters to the reader.

Holden Caulfield acts entirely like an adolescent, perhaps more so than any other adolescent portrayed in modern literature. At every turn he is a conflict of emotions: boastful, worried, annoyed, clumsy, and cynical, almost all at the same time. For example, as he leaves Pencey Prep, he shouts to his sleeping classmates "Sleep tight, ya morons!" then proceeds to trip and nearly break his neck falling down the stairs. The combination of teenage bravado and clumsiness is sad, funny, and true to life; for this reason, adolescents reading *The Catcher in the Rye* easily identify with its protagonist.

The Glass Children.

While Holden Caulfield is the most obviously isolated of Salinger's characters, isolation is also the pervading theme of the Glass stories. Even though the Glass siblings feel a close kinship, they are also incredibly isolated from one another. Seymour and Buddy, as the oldest children, form the apex of the clan. Zooey and Franny, as the youngest, form the base; they bear the brunt of their older siblings' histories and mistakes.

Zooey tells his sister that the Glass family is a family of freaks and that it is all the fault of their deceased brother, Seymour. The family members cannot relate to one another, nor can they relate to the average person they meet on the street, as Zooey points out. The Glass siblings have been raised to be constantly analytical and, as a result, they mentally tear apart every person they meet. This in turn means that they cannot form normal, noncompetitive relationships. They must always strive for something better, even if that thing is impossible to achieve and causes them to be alone.

In Max Ferguson's 1982 oil painting *Coffee Shop*, a lone man slumps on the counter burdened with the weight of his own thoughts. Likewise, Salinger's characters are loners, somewhat existentialist figures wandering through their cityscapes, often bereft of a quest to goad them along. They are the quintessential modern protagonists, so cerebral and incisive their constant mental exercises become a substitute for meaningful human interaction.

A Place in the World. After the 1960s Salinger attempted to withdraw from public view, expressing disdain for the industry of literary criticism and not feeling compelled to publish. The fact that Salinger's work—as little of it as there is—still continues to captivate new generations of readers is a testament to his writing abilities. The unfortunate side effect of his withdrawal from society, however, is a heightened interest in his work that he probably had neither intended nor anticipated.

BIBLIOGRAPHY

Alexander, Paul. *Salinger: A Biography*. Los Angeles: Renaissance Books, 1999.

Alsen, Eberhard. *Salinger's Glass Stories as a Composite Novel*. Troy, N.Y.: Whitston, 1983.

Bloom, Harold, ed. *J. D. Salinger: Modern Critical Views*. New York: Chelsea House, 1987.

French, Warren. *J. D. Salinger, Revisited*. Boston: Twayne Publishers, 1988.

Grunwald, Henry Anatole, ed. *Salinger: A Critical and Personal Portrait*, New York: Harper, 1962.

Hamilton, Ian. *In Search of J. D. Salinger*. New York: Random House, 1988.

Marsden, Malcolm M., comp. *If You Really Want to Know: A Catcher Casebook*, Chicago: Scott, 1963.

Maynard, Joyce. *At Home in the World*. New York: Picador USA, 1998.

Trosky, Susan M., ed. *Contemporary Authors: New Revision Series*. Vol. 39. Detroit: Gale Research, 1992.

Wenke, John Paul. *J. D. Salinger: A Study of the Short Fiction*. Boston: Twayne Publishers, 1991.

SOME INSPIRATIONS BEHIND SALINGER'S WORK

Although J. D. Salinger denied it, many of the facts in his own life seem to parallel those in the lives of his characters. Most striking is Salinger's withdrawal from society. Foreshadowing Salinger's actual move to New Hampshire, Holden Caulfield discusses the very same idea with Sally Hayes, suggesting that they could both leave the city, disappear to a cabin in Vermont, and live there happily for the rest of their lives.

The other large influence in Salinger's life is his interest in Eastern philosophy, which began in the 1940s at the Rama Krishna-Vivekanada Center in New York City. He first referred to it in his story "Teddy," about a boy who believes he is the reincarnation of a common Hindu man. In *The Catcher in the Rye* Holden meets an old acquaintance, Carl Luce, who is dating a Chinese woman, and he discusses why Eastern philosophy is better than Western philosophy.

Salinger's interest in Eastern philosophy is so great that it primarily dominates the rest of his published fiction. Seymour and Buddy Glass teach their worldview to their brothers and sisters. It becomes so ingrained in them that Zooey states it as the reason why Franny has a nervous breakdown and why he cannot eat a simple meal without reciting the Four Great Vows that Seymour taught him.

Eastern philosophy, suggested here by *Radha and Krishna Seated in a Grove* (Victoria and Albert Museum, London), is more than just a passing curiosity for Salinger. Like his characters, he seeks to transcend the cultural and intellectual blinders placed on him by Western society.

Salinger's Fight for Privacy

J. D. Salinger's *The Catcher in the Rye* was such a phenomenon that its popularity suddenly thrust him into the mainstream spotlight. By the time *Nine Stories* appeared in 1953, Salinger was considered the writer of the decade. However, the more popular Salinger became, the more he retreated from the limelight. During the 1960s, as his last collections of stories were being published, Salinger retreated to the New Hampshire countryside, bought some property, and began secluding himself from his fans.

At first, Salinger was willing to discuss his work with the public. This changed, however, after an interview with a local teenager. Shirley Blaney initially interviewed

Salinger's reclusive lifestyle has created as much of a sensation as his literary offerings. His Cornish, New Hampshire, home, shown here in a photograph from August 1987, is reputedly guarded against trespassers by two Doberman pinschers. Residents of the town offer their neighborly protection by often claiming they have never seen Salinger and do not know where he lives.

Salinger for the *New Hampshire Daily Eagle* newspaper but later sold the story to other newspapers. When Salinger learned that his story had been used in ways he had not expected, he became furious and vowed never to grant interviews again; for the most part he kept this vow.

Legal Battles. During the remaining decades of the twentieth century Salinger would be forced occasionally to emerge from his New Hampshire seclusion and engage in legal battles to protect his literary rights. During the 1970s an unauthorized edition of Salinger's early fiction, published by John Greenberg, appeared in California. Salinger considered his early writings unworthy of reprinting and wanted them to be forgotten. He considered their reproduction a violation of his privacy and his rights as an author.

One of the most signif-

In June 1999 Joyce Maynard auctioned fourteen letters that Salinger had written to her when she was eighteen. Due to the dearth of Salinger papers available, their appearance on the auction block created an unusual amount of interest.

icant violations of Salinger's privacy came when author Ian Hamilton attempted to use his letters in a biography. Salinger's letters had been on display at various universities, and Hamilton used them in the course of researching his book. Salinger did not want his letters used and filed a lawsuit to prevent this from happening. He even went so far as to copyright his letters so that they could not be reproduced without his consent, which he would never give. Hamilton was initially not allowed to use the letters at all, even in the form of paraphrasing. In 1987 the courts ruled that Hamilton could not use the content of the letters in any form whatsoever. Hamilton's book, *In Search of J. D. Salinger*, finally ap-

After the mid-1960s, Salinger was to become the phantom figure of American letters, the unapproachable recluse glimpsed only in unauthorized photographs.

peared in 1988. Instead of focusing on Salinger's life, it became a transcription of Hamilton's battles with Salinger.

Later Intrusions. Joyce Maynard, with whom Salinger shared a romantic relationship in the early 1970s, wrote her own autobiography, *At Home in the World* (1998). While the book is not entirely devoted to Salinger, it does describe her nine-month relationship with him in great detail, much to the dismay of Salinger's fans. Maynard also auctioned off a set of letters that Salinger had written to her during the course of their relationship. The letters were purchased by software entrepreneur Peter Norton, who said he would do with them whatever Salinger wished.

Maynard's autobiography was criticized as opportunism, but Salinger's reputation also fared badly. The fact that Salinger initiated the relationship with Maynard in response to her article "An Eighteen-Year-Old Looks Back on Life" while she was eighteen and he was in his early fifties, was seen in a somewhat unwholesome light.

The publicity over Salinger's letters has fueled the debate as to what is really private and what is public. Salinger's letters in the Princeton Archives are available for members of the public to see if they wish, yet Salinger would not let Hamilton use them in his biography. However, Salinger did not comment on the sale of Maynard's letters, which would seem to be more personal and private in nature. Presumably Salinger could have secretly bid on them himself and bought them back, but he chose not to do so.

Most likely, Salinger realizes that further public action will only bring him further into the public eye, which is what he has tried to avoid since the 1960s. He has consistently stated that he has no patience for anything that intrudes on his privacy and his writing time. Engaging in a public debate with Maynard over the content of her book would only bring more embarrassment upon himself, as well as an unending parade of reporters to disturb his privacy.

In addition, Salinger's daughter, Margaret Salinger, published a memoir about her life with her father, entitled *The Dream Catcher* (2000), detailing her relationship with her famous father and her unusual childhood. To date, Salinger's son, Matthew, an actor, has never commented on his father, short of saying that he loves him and respects his desire for privacy, and will therefore not discuss him with the public.

SOURCES FOR FURTHER STUDY

Alexander, Paul. *Salinger, A Biography*. Los Angeles: Renaissance Books, 1999.

Hamilton, Ian. *In Search of J. D. Salinger*. New York: Random House, 1988.

Maynard, Joyce. *At Home in the World: A Memoir*. New York: Picador USA, 1998.

Trosky, Susan M., ed. *Contemporary Authors: New Revision Series*. Vol. 39. Detroit: Gale, 1992.

Reader's Guide to Major Works

THE CATCHER IN THE RYE

Genre: Novel
Subgenre: Adolescent coming-of-age story
Published: New York, 1951
Time period: 1950s
Setting: New York City

Themes and Issues. Salinger's only published novel most strongly focuses on concepts to which almost any adolescent can relate: loneliness, awkwardness, and confusion. Holden Caulfield's world-weary cynicism also predates the modern adolescent cynicism portrayed in film and television for more than forty years.

The Plot. The novel opens with Holden sitting on a psychiatrist's couch telling the story of what happened to him during the weekend of his breakdown. The rest of the novel is a flashback, starting with the Saturday of a big football game at Pencey Prep, the school Holden attends. He has been notified that he is being kicked out of Pencey Prep, one of many schools from which he has been expelled for bad grades.

While Holden is deciding what to do, his roommate, Stradlater, announces that he is going on a date with Jane Gallagher, who was Holden's neighbor for one summer. Holden's memories of her are sweet and fond, and he worries that Stradlater will take advantage of her. When Stradlater returns, Holden has a fistfight with him over Jane. Holden ends up with a bloody lip and finally decides to leave Pencey Prep early and spend a few days in

New York City before his parents find out about his expulsion.

Holden checks into a seedy hotel in New York, trying to lay low until he can go home. He desperately misses his sister, Phoebe, and also nearly calls Jane Gallagher several times, but he finally settles on an old acquaintance, Sally Hayes. Sally agrees to meet him for a date that afternoon, but the date turns into a disaster. He is both attracted to and irritated by Sally, but

The Catcher in the Rye is Salinger's take on the Bildungsroman, a literary mode that traces a character's coming-of-age and struggle to define a place in the world. Holden Caulfield's academic frustrations, reflected here in A. Beltrame's *Schoolchildren Struggle Against Illiteracy*, and his desperate need for attention fuel his often rash behavior at school. In the hands of Salinger, Caulfield's typical adolescent confusions become universalized and accessible to all.

when he finally begins to tell her all of his feelings about school and people in general, Sally does not want to listen. When he finally suggests that they both run away to Vermont together and live in a log cabin, Sally tells him that he is crazy. Holden explodes and leaves.

After several more encounters, Holden finally sneaks back home and visits Phoebe. Phoebe is disappointed that he has been kicked out of school again and worries that their parents will be angry. Phoebe tells him that he is never happy with anything and that he does not know what he wants to do with his life. Holden replies that he wants to be a "catcher in the rye," protecting children from the danger and unhappiness in the world.

The next day Holden has finally decided to leave New York for good and he goes to Phoebe's school to say good-bye. Phoebe insists on going with him, and he realizes that he cannot leave after all. Holden takes his sister home, and the novel concludes with him in the psychiatrist's office, unsure whether he will return to school in the fall or not.

Analysis. The first chapter sets the tone for the entire novel with its blunt dialogue and Holden's matter-of-fact opinions about everything and everyone. On the first page, Holden declares that he is not about to recount a "David Copperfield" kind of story about misery and misfortune, one full of flowery language and sentimentality. He is going to speak the truth, at least as he sees it, and it does not concern him whether anyone else dislikes it.

Throughout the novel Holden reaches out and tries to establish connections with the people around him, but the only person with whom he succeeds is his nine-year-old sister, Phoebe. The novel is both about an adolescent struggling to deal with childhood tragedy—the death of his brother Allie—and about the time of adolescence itself, which is both awkward and confusing. When Holden proposes marriage to Sally he says he is completely sincere, but he is just as sincere moments later when he says that he never wants to see her again.

The Catcher in the Rye was an immediate suc-cess soon after publication, and it may be because of its overwhelming popularity that Salinger withdrew from public view a decade later. The novel continues to be the subject of attacks by censors who consider it indecent.

SOURCES FOR FURTHER STUDY

Bloom, Harold, ed. *J. D. Salinger: Modern Critical Views*. New York: Chelsea House, 1987.

French, Warren. *J. D. Salinger, Revisited*. Boston: Twayne Publishers, 1988.

Garrett, Agnes, and Helga P. McCue, eds. *Authors and Artists for Young Adults*. Vol. 2. Detroit: Gale Research, 1989.

Marsden, Malcolm M., comp.: *If You Really Want to Know: A Catcher Casebook*. Chicago: Scott, 1963.

FRANNY AND ZOOEY

Genre: Short fiction
Subgenre: Modernism
Published: New York, 1961
Time period: 1950s
Setting: Manhattan, New York

Themes and Issues. These two stories, "Franny" and "Zooey," essentially form one story, with the underlying theme being how Seymour Glass's suicide still haunts the Glass family. This book is Salinger's most spiritual; it deals with Franny's search for deeper meaning and Zooey's attempts to help his sister and himself deal with the past.

The Plot. "Franny" takes place on a Saturday as Franny Glass visits her boyfriend, Lane Coutell. Lane meets Franny at the train station and they go to eat lunch at Sickler's restaurant. Almost as soon as they sit down to lunch Franny feels nauseated, which irritates Lane, who thinks they will be late for a football game.

The entire story is a series of arguments between Franny and Lane over philosophical matters. As Franny gets sicker and sicker she constantly apologizes for ruining Lane's weekend, but Lane ignores her and is instead interested in the book she is carrying, *The Way of the Pilgrim*, a book about Christian prayer. As

Michael Mortimer Robinson's 1994 work *Grace* suggests the pensive Franny. On one hand freethinking and independent, she cannot escape the powerful influence Seymour had in shaping her insights. She struggles to fill the void created by his suicide.

Zooey finally talks to Franny and declares that the entire family is haunted by the ghost of Seymour, who instilled in them the Jesus prayer that Franny and all the others compulsively recite. Zooey tells her that if she is reciting the prayer in order to gain something, then that would be as bad as trying to gain something the traditional way. Franny finally breaks down and says that what she wants is to talk to Seymour. Zooey leaves and calls Franny on the telephone from Seymour's room. Pretending to be Buddy, he tells her that she should continue the prayer if she wants to. Franny knows it is Zooey on the phone, but his calling makes her feel better.

Analysis. "Franny" and "Zooey" are the last Glass stories to take place in chronological time, and they show the consequences of Seymour's and Buddy's unconventional teachings, as well as the lingering effects of Seymour's suicide upon the family. These two stories are also the most religious of Salinger's fiction. According to *The Way of the Pilgrim*, the Jesus prayer that the Glasses recite is supposed to be a final goal in and of itself. Franny is using the prayer, which she may be muttering in the restaurant at the time of her collapse, as an attempt to gain something—as a way to understand Seymour's suicide, or even possibly as a way to communicate with him again.

Franny and Zooey forms a sort of closure to the series. While other Glass stories were published after these, *Franny and Zooey* forms a chronological end to the Glass stories and perhaps shows that the Glass family finally finds some healing.

Franny walks to the rest room for a third time she passes out and wakes up in the restaurant manager's office. Lane goes to get a cab, and Franny begins to pray silently over and over like a character in her book.

"Zooey" takes place shortly after "Franny." Zooey Glass is taking a bath and rereading an old letter from his brother Buddy. He is interrupted by his mother, who is worried about Franny. She and Zooey debate whether they should try to contact Buddy or another brother, Waker, who is a priest. Zooey insists that Franny's problems are not religious. He also knows the book that Franny is reading because it came from Seymour's room.

SHORT FICTION

1953 Nine Stories
1961 Franny and Zooey
1963 Raise High the Roof
Beam, Carpenters, and
Seymour: An
Introduction

LONG FICTION

1951 The Catcher in the Rye

FRANNY
and ZOOEY

J.D. SALINGER

SOURCES FOR FURTHER STUDY

Poore, Charles. "Books of the Times: *Franny and Zooey*." *The New York Times*, September 14, 1961.

Trosky, Susan M., ed. *Contemporary Authors: New Revision Series*. Vol. 39. Detroit: Gale Research, 1992.

Wenke, John Paul. *J. D. Salinger: A Study of the Short Fiction*. Boston: Twayne Publishers, 1991.

RAISE HIGH THE ROOF BEAM, CARPENTERS, AND SEYMOUR: AN INTRODUCTION

Genre: Short fiction
Subgenre: Fictional biography
Published: New York, 1963
Time period: 1940s and 1950s
Setting: New York City

Themes and Issues. These two stories are an attempt for Buddy Glass, the Glass family writer and historian, to deal with the suicide of his older brother, Seymour. This is also Salinger's chance to try to explain Seymour to his readers, since Seymour appears alive only in the single story "A Perfect Day for Bananafish."

Eastern philosophy is a prevalent theme throughout the stories. One strong belief of Taoism, the Eastern philosophy of balance, is that the more one attempts to describe something, the further from the truth the description becomes, which is a clue to reading Buddy's memoir of his brother.

The Plot. "Raise High the Roof Beam, Carpenters" is the story of Seymour's wedding to Muriel. The wedding takes place in 1942, six years before Seymour's suicide. Buddy has been asked by his sister Boo Boo to attend in her place and arrives in New York just in time to make the wedding.

When he arrives, he and the other guests are waiting for the ceremony to begin, but it never does: Seymour has not shown up. Eventually the bride leaves, and everyone begins to leave for the reception. The matron of honor begins talking about Seymour's mental health, suggesting that Seymour should see a psychiatrist. Seymour's reason for stopping the wedding that day is that he is too happy to marry Muriel, which to the matron is utter nonsense.

The reception car gets stopped in a parade, and Buddy offers the party the use of the apartment that he, Seymour, and Boo Boo share. At the apartment Buddy finds Seymour's diary and begins reading it. Seymour writes that he wishes he made Muriel happier; he questions her motives for getting married but is greatly moved by them. Word finally comes that Seymour and Muriel have eloped, and everyone leaves. Buddy reads the last entry, which indicates that Seymour has accepted the idea of marriage after all.

"Seymour: An Introduction" is the longer of the two stories and the most difficult of Salinger's fiction. Told primarily as a reminiscence of the things that Buddy remembers about Seymour, Buddy ends up narrating the story in a rambling, somewhat abstract way. He offers a loving reminiscence of his brother but does so only in pieces that serve to make up the whole picture. In all Buddy's remembrances, such as of playing marbles with the kids down the street or of racing to the store

In "Raise High the Roof Beam, Carpenters," the ceremony and tradition of a wedding, glimpsed here in James Hayllar's *Happy Is the Bride the Sun Shines On*, become unnecessary obstacles to the joy and love of the freewheeling Seymour. To some of the guests, however, his failure to appear signals deeper problems than a quibble with social conventions.

for ice cream, Seymour is always the better marble player or the faster runner. Buddy finally realizes that he could spend the rest of his life trying to describe his brother and never get it quite right, and he decides to stop.

Analysis. As "Raise High the Roof Beam, Carpenters" begins, Buddy recounts a story that Seymour read to baby Franny in order to get her to sleep. It was a Taoist tale about a man who was so good at picking out horses that he couldn't see their common traits. Buddy shares this problem about Seymour. He considers Seymour the best at everything, and no matter how plainly he describes his brother, Seymour is still extraordinary.

Salinger has Buddy talk about Seymour not as an attempt to understand his suicide, but as a way to remember him. Seymour's suicide offers no answers, and Salinger doesn't try to suggest any. Despite the fantastical exploits and

wisdom of the Glass children, the fact that they can't comprehend Seymour's suicide makes them more realistic. "Seymour: An Introduction" is often regarded either as Salinger's masterpiece or as an incomprehensible and boring story. While it showcases Salinger's maturity and power as a writer, it also led to further criticism of his obsession with the Glass family and the fact that he wrote about nothing else.

SOURCES FOR FURTHER STUDY

Alsen, Eberhard. *Salinger's Glass Stories as a Composite Novel.* Troy, N.Y.: Whitston, 1983.

Bloom, Harold, ed. *J. D. Salinger: Modern Critical Views.* New York: Chelsea House, 1987.

French, Warren. *J. D. Salinger, Revisited.* Boston: Twayne Publishers, 1988.

Trosky, Susan M., ed. *Contemporary Authors: New Revision Series.* Vol. 39. Detroit: Gale Research, 1992.

Other Works

NINE STORIES (1953). Salinger's only published full collection of short fiction consists primarily of works previously published in *The New Yorker*. It contains Salinger's earliest Glass stories and other stories that he wrote. It is revealed in "Seymour: An Introduction" that many of these stories are written by Buddy Glass as part of his chronicles about his family.

The first Glass family story, "A Perfect Day for Bananafish," is the only story featuring Seymour Glass as a living character. Seymour and his wife, Muriel, are vacationing in Florida. While Muriel talks to her mother on the phone, Seymour is on the beach. Muriel's mother tells her that Seymour is dangerous and pompous. She notes that she has been talking to psychiatrists about Seymour and warns Muriel to be careful. Muriel has also talked to a psychiatrist at the hotel but is not worried.

The story switches to Seymour and Sybil, a little girl playing on the beach. Sybil finds Seymour, who begins to joke around with her. Seymour tells her about bananafish, which are fish that swim into holes in the ocean and eat so many bananas that they swell up and cannot get back out. Seymour and Sybil proceed to swim in the ocean looking for bananafish. Sybil claims to see one with six bananas in its mouth, and Seymour kisses her foot and returns to his hotel room. While Muriel is sleeping on one of the beds, Seymour climbs onto the other bed and commits suicide.

In "Just Before the War with the Eskimos," Ginnie Mannox and Selena Graff play tennis every day. Selena's family is rich and makes tennis balls, yet she never pays for anything, such as the girls' cab fare to and from the tennis courts. When Ginnie complains that it is

The offbeat and ultimately bleak vision of "A Perfect Day for Bananafish" unspools against the lighthearted and frolicsome setting of a day at the beach. The innocence of Sybil and the other vacationers, like the families in Arthur B. Davies's watercolor *Beach Scene with Female Bather Holding an Umbrella: Morning*, assumes a disquieting hint of menace as they pursue their diversions unaware of the impending tragedy.

Upset and confused, Lionel retreats to the boat in the short story "Down at the Dinghy." The innocence of childhood, suggested here by Stanhope Alexander Forbes's 1901 watercolor *Boy Fishing*, is threatened when Lionel's father becomes the target of an anti-Semitic slur.

unfair that she has to pay all the time, Selena makes a production out of having to pay Ginnie back. She tells Ginnie to wait in the living room while she gets the money.

Franklin, Selena's brother, then enters the room, complaining about his cut finger. When Ginnie tries to help Franklin take care of his finger, Franklin tells her that her sister is a snob because she did not answer his letters. Franklin tries to offer her a leftover chicken sandwich and talks about quitting the airplane factory where he used to work. He then brings her the sandwich and tells her to eat it. Franklin's friend Eric arrives, and Franklin leaves to get ready. When Selena finally arrives with the money, Ginnie tells her to forget about it and that she will come over later that night so they can do something together. On her way home, Ginnie contemplates throwing out her sandwich but changes her mind.

"Down at the Dinghy" features Boo Boo Tannenbaum, Seymour and Buddy Glass's married sister. Mrs. Snell and her maid, Sandra, are talking about Lionel, Boo Boo's child. They are worried that Lionel will tell Boo Boo what they said about his father. Lionel has run away to the dinghy, so Boo Boo makes a sandwich and takes it down to him.

Boo Boo attempts to lure Lionel out of the boat by pretending to be an admiral. Lionel refuses to let her aboard, even when Boo Boo promises to show him her secret military salute. Lionel finally starts crying and says he heard Sandra call his father a horrible name.

Boo Boo attempts to comfort him, and as the story closes they go into town to pick up his father.

"Teddy" was revealed in *Seymour: An Introduction* to be written by Buddy Glass, and the characters are thinly disguised versions of members of the Glass family. The story begins in a ship cabin with the parents arguing, while Teddy, a young boy, ignores his father's attempts to get him away from the porthole. His father sends him to retrieve his camera from his sister, Booper, who is playing on deck. After Teddy finds her, he sits down and begins writing in his journal.

Teddy is soon joined by Nicholson, who has heard of Teddy, and they begin discussing philosophy. Teddy believes he is the reincarnation of a Hindu man who stopped meditating because he met a woman and became distracted. He believes he has been reincarnated as an American because it will be harder to atone for his sins with all the distractions in the United States. Teddy also believes that he can predict when people will die. He goes on to suggest that death is not such a big deal, saying that, for example, he could go downstairs to the pool and there might not be any water in it, which could lead to an accident.

As Nicholson continues to question him, Teddy insists that he is late for an appointment to meet his sister at the pool. He finally leaves, and as Nicholson follows Teddy to the pool he hears the scream of a young girl, which sounds like it is coming from inside an empty pool.

Resources

J. D. Salinger's letters were the subject of much debate during the 1980s and 1990s. Despite Salinger's reclusiveness, there are still some sources of good information about the author and his work.

Princeton University Library Archives. Along with materials from *Story* magazine, which published some of Salinger's early work, are thirty-six letters and postcards from Salinger to various people at *Story* magazine. The majority of the letters are addressed to Whit Burnett, *Story*'s editor and a man who had a large influence on Salinger. The archives also house a collection of Ernest Hemingway's letters, and included in them is a letter Salinger wrote to Hemingway.

The Bananafish Server. One of the few long-standing Web sites devoted to J. D. Salinger and his work, it includes character and plot summaries and many resources for those doing research into Salinger's fiction. Also provided is a list of links to later Salinger articles and a discussion list for people to ask questions about Salinger's work. The Web site makes a conscious effort to conform to the wishes of Salinger's literary agents, Harold Ober Associates, and is probably the best Web site available for Salinger information (http://www.salinger.org)

Joyce Maynard's Home Page. The personal Web site of author Joyce Maynard has information on Maynard's life, her writing, and her memoir *At Home in the World*. It also contains a reprint of her article "An Eighteen-Year-Old Looks Back on Life," which was originally published in the April 23, 1972, edition of *The New York Times Magazine* and which initially inspired Salinger to contact her. (http://www.joyce-maynard.com)

KELLY ROTHENBERG

Carl Sandburg

BORN: January 6, 1878, Galesburg, Illinois
DIED: July 22, 1967, Flat Rock, North Carolina
IDENTIFICATION: Early- to mid-twentieth-century American journalist, poet, biographer, children's writer, folklorist, novelist, and platform performer known for giving free voice to the experiences and concerns of the common people.

The son of Swedish immigrants, Carl Sandburg identified with the American working class all his life. Born on the prairie and raised in Chicago, he was widely regarded as a midwestern writer, but his sympathies and his vision were much broader. His vigorous, unfettered poetic style was unconventional enough that some critics denied that it was poetic at all, even while others praised it. Sandburg admired Abraham Lincoln and wrote two monumental biographies of him. Although Sandburg's popularity as a writer peaked in the mid–twentieth century, he is still regarded as a significant poetic innovator and an important spokesman for American values.

The Writer's Life

Carl Sandburg was born on January 6, 1878, in Galesburg, Illinois, the second child of Swedish immigrants, August and Clara Sandburg. His hardworking, frugal, and undemonstrative father was a railroad blacksmith who struggled financially all his life. His mother was more affectionate and supportive.

Work, Wandering, and Education. Young Sandburg called himself Charles or Charlie, names he considered more American-sounding than Carl. He left school after the eighth grade to help support his family. His willing hands found many jobs in Galesburg—delivering newspapers and milk; handling ice; and working for a tinsmith, a potter, and a barber—all dead-end jobs.

In 1897 he left home seeking work but returned to Galesburg after three months. All the while he was watching and listening, learning about the lives of America's common people and forming strong convictions about the need for social reform. When the Spanish-American War broke out in 1898, Sandburg, bored and underemployed, joined the Sixth Illinois Volunteers, eventually landing in Puerto Rico. During his service, he wrote dispatches for the *Galesburg Evening Mail*.

After returning to Galesburg, Sandburg enrolled in Lombard College, where he distinguished himself as a basketball player, an orator, and a writer for college publications. He continued to work at odd jobs, becoming both a fireman and a salesman of stereoscopic slides. In 1902, after almost four years at Lombard, he left school without a degree. On the road again, he went east, selling stereoscopic slides and working briefly as a police reporter in New York City. He was arrested as a hobo in 1904 near Pittsburgh, and—despite his record of service in the war—he served ten days in jail.

Again in Galesburg, he resumed his friendship with his favorite pro-

In this studio portrait, a young Sandburg poses before a scene reminiscent of ancient Greece. The backdrop, most likely not chosen by Charlie, as he called himself at this time, presents an ironic statement in juxtaposition with Sandburg's later view of the past as "a bucket of ashes." The date of this photograph is unknown.

fessor at Lombard, Philip Green Wright, who published a pamphlet containing twenty-two of Sandburg's poems under the title *In Restless Ecstasy* in 1904. In 1906 Sandburg left Galesburg again, this time for Chicago. There he worked as a journalist and continued to struggle to establish himself as a poet and a lecturer. In 1907 he became an organizer for the Social Democratic Party in northeastern Wisconsin.

Marriage and a New Sense of Direction.

Tall, square shouldered, strong featured, and intense, Sandburg attracted women, but none who matched the ideal described in his poem "Dream Girl." Then in December 1907 on a visit to the state headquarters of the Social Democratic Party, he met Lilian Steichen, the sister of the noted photographer Edward Steichen. Immediately recognizing his dream girl, he got her address and wrote to her. In his letters he revealed his idealism and his doubts; in her replies she encouraged not only his party work but also his poetry.

Their correspondence blossomed into a courtship by mail, and on June 15, 1908, they were married. He called her Paula, and with her encouragement reverted to calling himself Carl. In 1909 the couple moved to Milwaukee, where Sandburg continued to work for the party and started writing for a newspaper. In 1910 a socialist, Emil Seidel, was elected mayor of Milwaukee, and Sandburg became his private secretary. In 1912 the couple moved to Chicago, where again Sandburg worked as a journalist.

In 1914, when Sandburg was thirty-six, he achieved his breakthrough as a poet. He had been writing poems in Chicago, and Paula submitted them to one magazine after another.

A very young looking twenty-year-old Sandburg poses in his Spanish-American War uniform in 1898. When he returned home at the war's end, he enrolled in Lombard College and was accepted even though he had never attended high school.

They decided to send a selection of these poems to a new, experimental magazine, *Poetry: A Magazine of Verse*. The editor, Harriet Monroe, bought nine poems, printing Sandburg's "Chicago" on the first page of the March issue. The poems drew immediate attention for their free-verse form and their uncompromising realism. Traditional critics denied that they were poetry at all, but at the end of the year, the board of the magazine—after consulting a dictionary for its definition of poetry—awarded Sandburg the two-hundred-dollar Levinson Prize for the best poems of the year.

Even more important than the money was the entry into the literary community that these Chicago poems earned for Sandburg.

Within a year, he became a friend of the poet Edgar Lee Masters and the novelist Theodore Dreiser—and soon after with the novelist Sinclair Lewis and the poets Ezra Pound, Robert Frost, and Amy Lowell. In 1916, with the assistance of Masters and Dreiser, Sandburg published *Chicago Poems*. Two more volumes followed, *Cornhuskers* in 1918 and *Smoke and Steel* in 1920. He was now established as an important and distinctive American poet.

Balancing Family and Career. The Sandburgs had a daughter, Margaret, in 1911; another, Janet, in 1916; and a third, Helga, in 1918. In 1918, after U. S. entry into World War I the previous year, Sandburg decided to become an overseas correspondent. Paula somewhat reluctantly supported him in his decision, and he was posted to Stockholm.

Sandburg returned to Chicago after the war, accepting positions as a reporter and then a film critic with the *Chicago Daily News*. With income from his newspaper job, his books, and his rapidly developing career as a platform performer, in which he gave poetry readings and public addresses, his family was increasingly prosperous. The extra income was needed, because in 1921 the Sandburgs' eldest daughter, Margaret, had the first of many epileptic seizures.

The family pursued every treatment medicine could offer to little avail. For Margaret and her sisters, Sandburg made up children's stories, which he published in 1922 and 1923, respectively, as *Rootabaga Stories* and *Rootabaga Pigeons*. Next he planned another book for children, one about the young Abe Lincoln. The project grew on him, and in 1926 he published the two volumes of *Abraham Lincoln: The Prairie Years*.

In 1926 the Sandburgs summered at a cottage on Lake Michigan. The next year they decided to build a house and move to Michigan permanently. Sandburg's income from his readings and lectures and especially from his publishing had become large enough that he could afford to leave the *Daily News*. The family's life now took a shape that it held for many years. Sandburg traveled often and widely, giving lectures and readings, collecting folk songs, and researching for his ongoing biographical work on Lincoln.

Between trips Sandburg worked at home on projects that tended to be large—notably his four-volume account of Lincoln's presidency, *Abraham Lincoln: The War Years* (1939), and his ambitious novel *Remembrance Rock* (1948). Paula cared for the three girls, two of whom needed special attention—Margaret for her

On the 150th anniversary of Abraham Lincoln's birth, Sandburg, whose four-volume account of Lincoln's presidency had been awarded a Pulitzer Prize, addressed a joint session of Congress. This photograph, taken on February 12, 1959, shows members of Congress listening to Sandburg eulogizing Lincoln. In addition to members of Congress, four members of the Supreme Court—Justices Potter Stewart, Charles E. Whitaker, William J. Brennan Jr., and John Marshall Harlan (front row, left to right)—were in attendance.

The many honors bestowed on Sandburg for his work ranged from medals presented by kings to honorary degrees from numerous schools across the United States. Here Sandburg accepts the Great Living American Award given to him by the U.S. Chamber of Commerce. The president of the Chamber, Erwin Canham, made the presentation on May 2, 1960.

epilepsy and Janet for mental retardation. Paula and the girls also developed a nationally prominent herd of dairy goats. In 1945 the family moved to the Connemara estate near Flat Rock, North Carolina, but their pattern of life remained largely unchanged except for a period of estrangement from Helga, who had married, divorced, and remarried.

Honors. Sandburg's honors began with the Levinson Prize for the best poems of 1914 in the magazine *Poetry*. In 1919 he shared the Poetry Society of America Prize, and in 1928 he was Phi Beta Kappa poet at Harvard University, and in 1943 Phi Beta Kappa poet at the College of William and Mary. In 1940 he won the Pulitzer Prize for history for his biography *Abraham Lincoln: The War Years* and in 1950 the Pulitzer Prize for poetry for his collection *Complete Poems* (1950).

Sandburg received honorary degrees from many schools in his home state, including Lombard and Knox Colleges in Galesburg, Northwestern University, the University of Chicago, Augustana College, and the University of Illinois. He also received degrees from a host of colleges and universities across the United States, as well as from Uppsala in Sweden.

Sandburg was elected to the American Academy of Arts and Letters in 1940 and in 1952 received the academy's Gold Medal Award for history and biography. The next year he received the Poetry Society of America's gold medal. In 1959 he received a medal from King Gustav VI of Sweden. On February 12, 1959—the one hundred fiftieth anniversary of the birth of Abraham Lincoln—Sandburg addressed a joint session of the U. S. Congress. In September of 1964, Sandburg received the Presidential Medal of Freedom at the White House.

On July 22, 1967, after two years of failing health, Carl Sandburg died peacefully at his home. His last word was his wife's name—Paula.

HIGHLIGHTS IN SANDBURG'S LIFE

1878	Carl Sandburg is born on January 6 in Galesburg, Illinois.
1891	Leaves school after eighth grade; takes odd jobs to help support his family.
1898	Enlists in Sixth Illinois Volunteers and serves in Puerto Rico during Spanish-American War; returns to Galesburg and enrolls at Lombard College.
1902	Leaves Lombard before graduation; works at odd jobs, selling stereographic photographs and traveling around the country.
1908	Serves as an organizer for the Social Democratic Party in Wisconsin; marries Lilian "Paula" Steichen.
1909	Works as a newspaper reporter in Milwaukee.
1910	Serves for two years as a private secretary to Emil Seidel, the socialist mayor of Milwaukee.
1911	First daughter, Margaret, is born.
1912	Sandburg begins work as a newspaper reporter in Chicago.
1914	Publishes nine "Chicago Poems" in *Poetry*; wins Levinson Prize for that magazine's best poems of the year; forms the first of many literary friendships.
1916	Publishes his first full-length volume of poetry, *Chicago Poems*; second daughter, Janet, is born.
1917	Sandburg is briefly unemployed; joins *Chicago Daily News* as a reporter.
1918	Travels to Stockholm, Sweden, as a correspondent for the Newspaper Enterprise Association; third daughter, Helga, is born.
1919	Sandburg returns to *Daily News* and covers race riots in Chicago and then works as film critic.
1920	Performs at Cornell College in Iowa, the first of many college performances.
1922	Publishes *Rootabaga Stories*.
1926	Publishes *Abraham Lincoln: The Prairie Years*.
1927	Resigns from *Daily News* and settles on the Michigan dunes.
1939	Publishes *Abraham Lincoln: The War Years*.
1940	Wins Pulitzer Prize for history; is elected to American Academy of Arts and Sciences.
1945	Moves to Connemara, an estate near Flat Rock, North Carolina.
1950	Publishes *Complete Poems*; wins Pulitzer Prize for poetry.
1956	University of Illinois pays fifty thousand dollars for four tons of Sandburg papers.
1967	Sandburg dies on July 22, at Connemara.

The Writer's Work

Carl Sandburg's works include journalism, essays, poetry, children's literature, biography, histories, fiction, and two collections of folk songs. He is best known as a poet and biographer. As a poet he treated new subjects in a new light and in new forms; as a biographer he wrote accounts that were exhaustive yet accessible. To both poetry and biography he brought a journalist's concern for clear, factual writing.

Themes in Sandburg's Poetry. Sandburg was a popular poet, not an abstract philosopher or a critical theorist. He wrote of the people, from the people, and to the people. Sandburg wrote about working men and women—steelworkers, teamsters, farmers, bricklayers, writers, cashiers, salesgirls, prostitutes, dancers, ditch diggers, ice handlers, union members—and the unemployed. His works concern Native Americans, African Americans, Italian Americans, and Polish Americans. He wrote about war—about patriotism, about futility and waste, about the work of war. He wrote about the class struggle—about the patience and growing self-awareness of the masses and about the enemies of the people—millionaires, bosses, evangelists, lawyers, and the hangman.

Sandburg wrote about love—wistful, frustrated, or fulfilled; about parenthood—hopeful, despairing, grief stricken; about neighbors; and about other people's relationships and families and about his own. His works speak of the world around the people—about skyscrapers, factories, tombs, railroads, streetcars, and excursion boats; about soil, cinders, and ashes; about harbors, streams, and pools; about the city, small towns, and the prairie; about the moon, the stars, and sunsets; and about smoke, mist, and—most famously—fog.

Sandburg was very much a poet of his present, describing the world as it was, immediate and concrete. He regarded wistfulness for what might be as no more substantial than nostalgia for what was—and "the past," as he said in an often-quoted line, "is a bucket of ashes." In 1914, when his poems first drew national and international attention, his straightforward presentation of the details of the lives of ordinary people was revolutionary.

Technique in Sandburg's Poetry. At least as revolutionary as the themes of Sandburg's poetry were the language and the forms he used to present the things he saw. At a time when people were accustomed to a formal,

Sandburg's most famous works are his two monumental biographies of Lincoln. The first of these, the two-volume *Abraham Lincoln: The Prairie Years,* was published in 1926. This photograph, taken in 1960 at the Chicago Historical Society Museum, shows Sandburg seated at a desk that belonged to Lincoln. Looming above Sandburg is the massive "rail-splitter" portrait of Lincoln that typifies his prairie years.

even slightly archaic, poetic diction, Sandburg used slang such as "pal," "bunkshooter," "hunky," and "a bum on the bumpers." This language provided energy, immediacy, and authenticity; it precluded sentimentality. As revolutionary as his diction was Sandburg's attitude toward poetic form. Sandburg distrusted rhyme, believing that it misled poets into saying what they did not mean.

For much the same reason Sandburg avoided metric regularity, instead writing free verse. This practice earned him the jibe from Robert Frost that writing free verse is like playing tennis without a net and caused less articulate critics to question whether Sandburg's work was poetry at all. Yet Sandburg's work was neither arbitrary nor careless. He told an interviewer that he spent a great deal of time finding the right words, the right lines for his poems. The published version of "Prairie" was a fourteenth draft, he said. The long poem "Good Morning, America" took him three years to complete. If one reads Sandburg's poems aloud, as he himself did to audiences for more than forty years, one can hear the "rightness" of his lines.

Sandburg's Prose. Ironically enough for a writer who had declared that "the past is a bucket of ashes," Sandburg was caught by the historical presence of Abraham Lincoln, whose antecedents and ideals seemed so much like his own. To his monumental biographies of Lincoln—and his historical novel *Remembrance Rock*—Sandburg brought a poet's imaginative intuition and a journalist's impulse to report the facts. He did not write academic history;

even in the biographies he did not document his copious research, and he allowed himself to speculate when he encountered gaps in the historical record. He did make history accessible to the common reader—in sometimes almost overwhelming detail—in much same way that he made poetry accessible.

BIBLIOGRAPHY

Callahan, North. *Carl Sandburg: His Life and Works.* University Park: Pennsylvania State University Press, 1986.

Crowder, Richard. *Carl Sandburg.* New York: Twayne Publishers, 1964.

Durnell, Hazel B. *The America of Carl Sandburg.* Washington, D.C.: University Press of Washington, D.C., 1965.

Golden, Harry. *Carl Sandburg.* Cleveland, Ohio: World, 1961.

Andre Lhote's painting *L'Escale* (The Port of Call) (Musée National d'Art de Moderne, Paris, France) presents the world of prostitutes, women who live on the fringes of society, and evokes one of Sandburg's "people," the fallen woman in his poem "Soiled Dove."

Haas, Joseph, and Gene Lovitz. *Carl Sandburg: A Pictorial Biography*. New York: Putnam, 1967.

Niven, Penelope. *Carl Sandburg: A Biography*. New York: Charles Scribner's Sons, 1991.

Perry, Lilla S. *My Friend Carl Sandburg: The Biography of a Friendship*. Metuchen, N.J.: Scarecrow Press, 1981.

Sandburg, Helga. *A Great and Glorious Romance: The Story of Carl Sandburg and Lilian Steichen*. New York: Harcourt Brace Jovanovich, 1978.

Sutton, William A., ed. *Carl Sandburg Remembered*. Metuchen, N.J.: Scarecrow Press, 1979.

Van Doren, Mark. *Carl Sandburg: With a Bibliography of Sandburg Materials in the Collections of the Library of Congress*. Washington, D.C.: Library of Congress, 1969.

SOME INSPIRATIONS BEHIND SANDBURG'S WORK

Carl Sandburg said that he tried to write the books he wished he could have read when he was growing up. Sandburg was deeply influenced by witnessing the experiences of the common people among whom he lived and worked and especially by his father's difficult struggle to make a living. His ear was attuned to the language and the rhythms of common speech, and his eye was focused on images from the lives of ordinary people, urban or rural.

Sandburg regarded himself and was regarded by others as a revolutionary poet rather than a traditionalist, yet much of his work shows the influence of Walt Whitman, for whose poetry Sandburg had a lifelong enthusiasm. Whitman's loose free verse forms, his rhetorical devices of cataloging and repetition, his use of common speech and images from common life, and his democratic vision all have counterparts in Sandburg's verse. Sandburg also spoke of the influence of Emily Dickinson on his shorter lyrics, an influence to be seen in the rhythms, the vivid images, and the intense emotional content of these poems.

As a boy and a young man on the prairie, Sandburg knew people who had known Abraham Lincoln. He heard Robert Todd Lincoln speak in Galesburg on the thirty-eighth anniversary of the Abraham Lincoln–Stephen A. Douglas debate at Knox College, and he decided that the son was not worthy of the father. Sandburg's great empathy for Lincoln was a strength and perhaps also a weakness of his Lincoln biographies.

Sandburg himself listed three people who influenced him most strongly in his life: his Lombard College professor Philip Green Wright; his wife, Paula Steichen Sandburg; and her brother, the photographer Edward Steichen.

Six months after Sandburg's death, his wife, Lilian "Paula" Sandburg, recalls earlier years as she views a 1923 photograph of herself and Sandburg. This photograph was taken on January 9, 1968, at the Hallmark Gallery in New York City during a six-week exhibit of Sandburg's manuscripts, books, and letters.

Carl Sandburg
the Platform Performer

In 1890 twelve-year-old Charlie (Carl) Sandburg entered a declamation contest sponsored by the Junior Christian Endeavor Society. He memorized a speech on temperance and on the evening of the contest spoke to an audience of perhaps two hundred, including his father and mother. Well into his speech, he became self-conscious and suddenly forgot the words he had memorized. Cued by the prompter, he struggled in humiliation to the end of the speech, stung by the laughter of the witnesses to his shame. He knew they weren't laughing at his ideas, they were laughing at him, and he vowed he would never again earn such laughter. He worked consciously to develop his memory, reciting facts and poetry while he worked at odd jobs.

Practice and Persistence. Ten years later, Charles Sandburg, by then a Lombard College student, joined the Eurosophian Society, which was devoted to the arts of elocution and oratory. Each year, Lombard held the Swan Oratorical Contest, with a prize of fifteen dollars. Sandburg wrote a speech, which he practiced faithfully, but on the night of the contest, he once again forgot his lines. Undeterred, for the 1901 contest he prepared another speech, on the nineteenth-century British social reformer John Ruskin. Fired with enthusiasm for Ruskin's social ideals, he delivered his speech with fervor—and with no mistakes. He won first place. More important than the fifteen-dollar prize was the self-confidence he gained.

Inspired by early failure and subsequent success, Sandburg was increasingly interested in oratory. In the era before radio, television, and motion pictures, he had many opportunities to hear lecturers, and he studied their techniques: their diction, their delivery, and their power to influence audiences—as well as their ability to make money at lecturing. He was particularly impressed by the American writer, editor, and printer Elbert Hubbard, as a man, as a speaker, and as the leader of a cultural movement in handicrafts and artistic printing.

Platform Performance. During the summer of 1906, Sandburg actively prepared for a career as a touring lecturer, preparing presentations on Walt Whitman, written language, and socialism. He performed on several midwestern platforms but earned little. He had an illustrated brochure printed up advertising "Charles A. Sandburg, Lecturer and Orator." The picture shows Sandburg as a darkly handsome, brooding young man with strong features. During the winter he prepared lectures on new topics.

In 1907, with Elbert Hubbard's encouragement, Sandburg delivered his lecture on Walt Whitman, "An American Vagabond," at Hubbard's annual Convention of the

This picture shows Sandburg in his later years singing folk songs to his own accompaniment. A radio station microphone is beside the microphone in front of Sandburg, indicating his performance is being broadcast. The date and location of this photograph are unknown.

Elect. The lecture was a great success, and Sandburg was asked to speak twice again during the convention. Despite the applause of the national audience and the support of Hubbard himself, relatively few bookings for future lecture engagements materialized, but Sandburg remained optimistic about his future as lecturer and orator even as he undertook a new career as an organizer for the Social Democratic Party in Wisconsin. As an organizer, he addressed audiences large and small, in forums both formal and informal, on social, economic, and political issues. He supported himself with the dues paid by recruits he persuaded to join the party.

Poetic Performance. Years later, in 1920, when Sandburg had established himself as a poet, he was invited to give a reading of his poetry at Cornell College in Iowa for a fee of one hundred dollars. He accepted. After about an hour of reading, he began to sing folk songs, accompanying himself on his guitar. He and his audience got along so well that Sandburg kept talking and reading and singing with some of them elsewhere long after the formal performance was over. Sandburg was invited back to Cornell repeatedly.

Sandburg's career as a reader and lecturer developed rapidly during 1920 and afterward, as he performed at many colleges and other venues. Although his trips and later his extended tours took him from away from home, they offered him a variety of benefits. In addition to the fees he earned, he found new readers to buy his books. Always the wanderer, he enjoyed the travel that lecture tours entailed. He liked making new friends, learning new songs, and finding new materials for his research on Abraham Lincoln. Wherever he went he could watch films for his columns as the film critic of the *Chicago Daily News*. On one trip, he went west, visiting, among

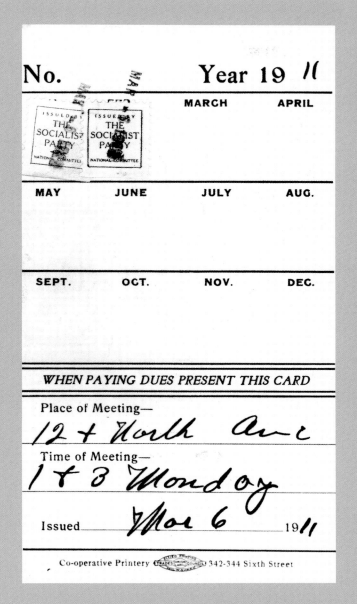

other places, Hollywood, California, where he had the unique pleasure of playing charades one evening with Charlie Chaplin.

For a typical performance in any year from the early 1920's to the early 1960's, an audience—often made up mostly of students—would gather. Onto the stage before them would come a tall, lean, erect man wearing a suit, a white shirt, and a bow tie. He would be carrying a guitar, which he would lay aside. Over his forehead would be a long shock of hair—strikingly white in his later years.

Sandburg would recite some of his poems—some quite familiar to his audience, some not so familiar—and talk about the poems. He might tell a Rootabaga story or speak about Lincoln. Then he would take off his coat, pick up his guitar, and sing folk songs—in many cases well-known songs he had popularized in his books *The American Songbag* (1927) and *The New American Songbag* (1950). In such performances Sandburg offered to his audiences his most characteristic, most polished, and most authentic artistic creation—the public persona of Carl Sandburg: multitalented, many faceted, yet in the performance, integrated and whole.

SOURCES FOR FURTHER STUDY

Durnell, Hazel B. *The America of Carl Sandburg*. Washington, D.C.: University Press of Washington, D.C., 1965.

Niven, Penelope. *Carl Sandburg: A Biography*. New York: Charles Scribner's Sons, 1991.

Sutton, William A., ed. *Carl Sandburg Remembered*. Metuchen, N.J.: Scarecrow Press, 1979.

ABRAHAM LINCOLN: THE PRAIRIE YEARS (2 volumes)

ABRAHAM LINCOLN: THE WAR YEARS (4 volumes)

>   **Genre:** Nonfiction
>   **Subgenre:** Biography
>   **Published:** New York, 1926 and 1939
>   **Time period:** 1776–1865
>   **Setting:** Midwestern United States; Washington, D.C.

Themes and Issues. Carl Sandburg was born little more than a dozen years after Abraham Lincoln died. He grew up on land Lincoln knew, among people who knew Lincoln. If Lincoln was forever gone, laid in his cool tomb, he was also tantalizingly close, touched in places, artifacts, and written words; in the memories of the people; and in a sympathetic imagination. It was important to recapture Lincoln truly, Sandburg believed, because Lincoln's vision of America, a nation of the people, was needed in the confusion of the 1920s.

Sandburg's biographies are monumental. The four-volume account of the war years is longer than the Bible including the Apocrypha, and longer than the collected works of William Shakespeare. Most of this length comes from the facts Sandburg assembled by exhaustive research. Some of it comes in lyrical passages—prose poems, really—and some comes in the form of apocryphal anecdotes or—especially in the first two volumes—in pure speculation where no evidence was available. Although the six volumes of Sandburg's Lincoln biography were well researched, they presented little or nothing that was new to history. The few errors in Sandburg's account were generally corrected in later editions or in the one-volume condensation published as *Abraham Lincoln: The Prairie Years and the War Years* in 1954. Sandburg's Lincoln biographies are not documented.

Antoine Chintreuil's nineteenth-century painting *L'Espace* (Space) (Musee d'Orsay, Paris, France) embodies the American prairie that Abraham Lincoln would have known. The wide-open spaces and a house alone with no others nearby captures the vastness of the land Lincoln would later struggle to hold together as one nation.

The Text. In writing his biography, Sandburg was a good reporter, asking the journalist's questions: who, what, where, when, why, how? Sandburg presents the evidence in a series of usually short chapters and often leaves readers to draw their own conclusions. The resulting picture of Lincoln resembles that of Sandburg himself: largely self-educated, amiable yet self-contained, full of sadness, full of laughter, seemingly simple and yet deeply complex, a practical man and an idealist, a common man who was more than common, a lover of language, a lover of the people, and a believer in the people.

This photograph taken during the Civil War at Fredericksburg, Virginia, at some of the bloodiest ground in history, has been titled "That Terrible Stone Wall." The Confederate soldiers, massed in the Sunken Road behind the stone wall, held off wave after wave of attacking Union troops, killing thousands. Finally, as this photograph, taken by a Union officer, Captain Russell, shows, the Confederate soldiers were swept from the Sunken Road behind the wall. The horrors of the Civil War had a deep affect on Abraham Lincoln and strengthened his will to keep America undivided.

Analysis. Biography is not a precise reproduction of the past but an interpretation, depending on the selection of material and the coherence given to it. Sandburg's biography is so comprehensive that some readers found in it no principle of selection, no interpretation. Yet there can be discerned an evolving theme—the growth of a leader who shepherded the American people through the crisis of the Civil War. If, as president, Lincoln was at times devious, at times almost dictatorial, it was not in the interest of self-aggrandizement but always in the interests of the nation and democracy.

Sandburg's biography can be seen to have a second subject—the American people, who were challenged to develop into a nation worthy of their great leader. The biography's model of democratic leadership and democratic responsibility in a time of crisis was highly relevant in the era of the New Deal, when Sandburg wrote *Lincoln: The War Years*. Not coincidentally, Sandburg was a strong supporter of the Franklin D. Roosevelt administration.

Sandburg's Lincoln biographies were appreciated by the critics and very popular with the reading public. Particularly in the one-volume condensation of 1954, Sandburg's biography remains one of the most accessible accounts of Lincoln's life.

SOURCES FOR FURTHER STUDY

Callahan, North. *Carl Sandburg: Lincoln of Our Literature.* New York: New York University Press, 1970.

Commager, Henry Steele. "Lincoln Belongs to the People." *Yale Review* 29 (Winter 1940).

Nevins, Allan. "Sandburg as Historian." *Journal of the Illinois State Historical Society* 45 (Winter 1952).

COMPLETE POEMS

Genre: Poetry
Subgenre: Lyrics and long poems
Published: New York, 1950
Time period: Early twentieth century
Setting: United States

Themes and Issues. Almost everyone who knows anything about Sandburg's poetry knows that Sandburg wrote a poem beginning "Hog Butcher for the World." This is the first line of Sandburg's most well-known poem, "Chicago," and so it is the first line of the March 1914 issue of *Poetry* magazine; the first line of Sandburg's first serious collection of poems (*Chicago Poems*); and the first line of Sandburg's *Complete Poems*.

For readers who learned about poetry by reading the work of nineteenth-century American poets such as William Cullen Bryant and Henry Wadsworth Longfellow or of British poets from the same era, such as Alfred, Lord Tennyson; Robert Browning; and Algernon Charles Swinburne—this first line is a slap in the face. Harriet Monroe, the editor of *Poetry*, said that when she first read this opening, it shocked her. She read on and became an enthusiastic advocate of Sandburg's poetry. Not every reader got past that initial slap in the face. "Chicago" is an excellent example of one of Sandburg's characteristic attitudes as a poet.

The Poems. The poem "Chicago" opens with a series of epithets—neither pretty nor formal but original and true. Then follows a series of admissions of the city's faults and a further series of observations, actually boasts, about the city.

POETRY

1916   Chicago Poems
1918   Cornhuskers
1920   Smoke and Steel
1922   Slabs of the Sunburnt West
1926   Selected Poems of Carl Sandburg
1928   Good Morning, America
1930   Early Moon
1936   The People, Yes
1943   Home Front Memo (verse and prose)
1946   Chicago Poems: Poems of the Midwest
1950   Complete Poems
1960   Wind Song
1960   Harvest Poems, 1910–1960
1963   Honey and Salt
1978   Breathing Tokens, ed. Margaret Sandburg
1983   Ever the Winds of Chance, Margaret Sandburg and George Hendrick, eds.

LONG FICTION

1948   Remembrance Rock

NONFICTION

1919   The Chicago Race Riots

1926   Abraham Lincoln: The Prairie Years (2 volumes)
1929   Steichen the Photographer
1932   Mary Lincoln: Wife and Widow (with Paul M. Angle)
1938   A Lincoln and Whitman Miscellany
1939   Abraham Lincoln: The War Years (4 volumes)
1942   Storm over the Land: A Profile of the Civil War
1944   The Photographs of Abraham Lincoln
1949   Lincoln Collector: The Story of Oliver R. Barrett's Great Private Collection
1953   Always the Young Strangers
1954   Abraham Lincoln: The Prairie Years and the War Years
1957   The Sandburg Range
1959   "Address Before a Joint Session of Congress, February 12, 1959"
1968   The Letters of Carl Sandburg, ed. Herbert Mitgang

CHILDREN'S LITERATURE

1922   Rootabaga Stories
1923   Rootabaga Pigeons
1928   Abe Lincoln Grows Up
1930   Potato Face
1955   Prairie-Town Boy
1967   The Wedding Procession of the Rag Doll and the Broom Handle and Who Was in It

EDITED TEXTS

1927   The American Songbag
1950   The New American Songbag

CARL SANDBURG

THE PEOPLE, YES

A HARVEST BOOK

Although the effect is not really to rationalize Chicago's faults, the poem as a whole is celebratory, an affirmation of the city's energy, its productiveness, its resilience, its ability to make and remake itself and still remain essentially itself.

In the *Complete Poems* are many such celebrations of things and events and people not conventionally celebrated. For example, the little poem "Gone" celebrates a "fast" girl named Chick Lorimer, certainly one of the more recognizable characters of American poetry. The poem opens with the unresolved ambiguity of the assertion that everyone in town (any of the small towns Sandburg knew so well) "loved" Chick Lorimer. At the end of the poem, the reader is left with the wistfulness of five or fifty men who miss her but also with the gallant image of Chick moving on—to better things, one hopes—"with her little chin / thrust ahead of her."

Sandburg also writes poems of protest—for example, "Soiled Dove," another of his Chicago poems, which describes a singer and dancer who falls when she marries a corporation lawyer and becomes a prostitute. A later poem, "The Hangman at Home" speculates about what the hangman must think about after work—about whether he jokes about rope or whether it is easy for him to see the innocence of a sleeping baby.

Poignant despair flavors "Mag," another protest poem, which asks what kind of country allows a husband and father to wish he had never had a child or had never met his wife. The anger of "To a Contemporary Bunkshooter," originally directed explicitly at the evangelist Billy Sunday, is yet another example of forthright protest, this time against pious—and profitable—hypocrisy.

Sandburg is also an ironist; in "Southern Pacific" he observes a financier and one of his lowest employees lying finally in identical graves. In "Grass" he shows how quickly the grass obliterates any trace of heroism on battlefields such as Waterloo and Gettysburg and Verdun. Sandburg is also a lyricist, singing at length the praises of the prairie in the poem "Prairie." One of many more examples of Sandburg's lyric voice is the little poem "On a Railroad Right of Way."

When *Poetry* first published Sandburg's poems, a rival magazine, the *Dial*, criticized their "ragged lines." *The Dial* was not alone. Even the judges who awarded Sandburg the Levinson Prize had to be reassured by a dictionary definition that poetry was "not necessarily arranged in the form of measured verse or numbers." Many commentators observed that Sandburg's free verse often looks like Whitman's. His rhythms are fluid, colloquial, or rhetorical and at their best are actually more varied and expressive than Whitman's. Sandburg is a notoriously uneven poet, however, and if a critic wishes to deny a piece like "Sleepyheads" or much of "Many Hats" the title of poetry, the critic may have a case.

The image in Diego Rivera's powerful mural *Blood of the Revolutionary Martyrs Fertilizing the Earth* (*Sangre de los martirios*),1926–1927, evokes Sandburg's poem "Southern Pacific." While Rivera's mural in the chapel at the Universidad Autonoma Chapingo in Chapingo, Mexico, is a tribute to the martyrs of the Mexican revolution, Sandburg's poem is an ironic statement on death's role as an equalizer of classes. Rich, poor, martyr, coward, all end up fertilizing a small plot of earth.

Sandburg's approach to poetic form may be well exemplified in one of his best-known poems, "Fog." The poem is composed of a half-dozen lines that Sandburg jotted down while waiting to interview a Chicago juvenile court judge for a newspaper article. Sandburg called the poem a "free-going, independent American Hoku." It certainly has the spirit of traditional haiku, with its close and imaginative perception of nature—and indeed, if one were to substitute the poem's first two words, "the fog," for the pronoun "it" at the beginning of the third line, lines three, four, and five of "Fog" would correspond exactly to the seventeen syllable form of traditional haiku.

Sandburg was not after traditional form, however; his long apprenticeship in poetry had taught him to avoid the triteness of expression and the falseness of feeling that traditional forms seemed to entail. His poem starts earlier and runs longer than the traditional form in order to present more fully and accurately both physical detail and emotional response. The inordinate popularity of this poem may have irked Sandburg; he took particular pleasure in parodying it within his family: "De fog come on itti bitti kitti footsies."

Analysis. Early in 1908 Sandburg wrote to Lilian Steichen that he planned to abandon poetry in order to work for social reform. She asked whether he could not do both. For most of the next sixty years, Sandburg did try to do both, and the tension between his social and his aesthetic impulses persisted. After he published *Chicago Poems* in 1916, his friend the poet Amy Lowell feared that the propagandist might crowd out the poet in Sandburg's work.

With his reporter's eye for what is and his reformer's zeal for what ought to be, Sandburg doggedly pursued his interest in discovering what really is American about America. The poet William Carlos Williams hurt Sandburg when he suggested in his review of *Complete Poems* that Sandburg should have concentrated more on what might be poetic about poetry. The criticism is just. Sandburg did not have a theory of poetry or a consistent poetic voice, as Whitman or Frost or Williams himself did. However, if the test of poetry is, as the eighteenth-century British poet and critic Alexander Pope said, to present "what oft was thought, but ne'er so well expressed," Sandburg wrote many passages and many poems that meet that test.

SOURCES FOR FURTHER STUDY

Allen, Gay Wilson. *Carl Sandburg*. Minneapolis: University of Minnesota Press, 1972.

Hoffman, Daniel. *"Moonlight Dries No Mittens": Carl Sandburg Reconsidered*. Washington, D.C.: Library of Congress, 1979.

Williams, William Carlos. "Carl Sandburg's *Complete Poems*." *Poetry: A Magazine of Verse* 78 (September 1951).

Wilson, Edmund. "The All-Star Literary Vaudeville." *The Shores of Light: A Literary Chronicle of the 1920s and 30s*. Boston: Northeastern University Press, 1985.

Other Works

ALWAYS THE YOUNG STRANGERS

(1953). In his seventies, Carl Sandburg wrote *Always the Young Strangers*, an account of the first twenty years of his life, ending with his return to Galesburg after the Spanish-American War. In the poem that serves as the book's epigraph, he says that he wrote the book to recapture the who, what, when, and where of his youth—and especially the how. *Always the Young Strangers* is a story about growing up but not a story about the education of a young man that comes to some sort of crisis or illustrates an abstract moral scheme.

Like Sandburg's Lincoln books, this autobiography develops through the patient accretion of facts. The book's organization is chronological; events are described simply, clearly, and honestly in a lively and immediate way; the language is unpretentious. Sandburg's autobiography is essentially American, but readers from different cultures have also recognized in it the patterns of their own development. Much less ambitious than *Remembrance Rock*, *Always the Young Strangers* is, however, a more successful work.

THE AMERICAN SONGBAG (1927). Like the body of Sandburg's poetry, his Lincoln biographies, and his novel *Remembrance Rock*, *The American Songbag* tries to capture the American spirit, this time in the words and tunes of "varied human characters and communities . . . thousands of original singing Americans," as Sandburg described them in his introduction. *The American Songbag* included 280 songs together with the songs' histories, sometimes including the circumstances under which Sandburg learned them.

Sandburg had been learning songs since his days as a hobo, from friends, acquaintances, and strangers—sources as diverse as Mary Baker Eddy, founder of the Christian Science Church, and the iconoclastic social critic H. L. Mencken. The songs were as diverse as their sources: "Barbra Allen," "Git Along Little Dogies," "The Boll Weevil Song," "Blow the Man Down," and "Hallelujah, I'm a Bum."

Editing *The American Songbag* was a demanding task; Sandburg said the book almost killed him. However, the songs it contains have shaped the understanding of America held by generations since 1927.

THE CHICAGO RACE RIOTS (1919). During the summer of 1919, there was racial tension across the United States. A former itinerant laborer and political organizer, Sandburg was uniquely prepared to report on conditions in Chicago. He gathered the facts on housing, on infant mortality, on bombings and lynchings, and on a host of injustices. His reporting was thorough and balanced, placing Chicago's experience in its national context.

Sandburg felt that the causes of the problems on which he reported were economic in nature. The solutions were education, job training, and the guarantee of the civil rights envisioned in the Declaration of Independence and confirmed in Civil War bloodshed. Sandburg began his investigation before the

In *The Chicago Race Riots,* a collection of articles Sandburg wrote during the 1919 race riots, he chronicled the problems and conditions that led to the racial violence. This photograph taken on September 1, 1919, shows young white children cheering outside a black family's residence that they had set afire.

city exploded in violence. This collection of his articles published afterward may not have been widely enough distributed; in any case, it was still timely when it was reissued in 1969.

REMEMBRANCE ROCK (1948). In 1943 Sandburg agreed with Metro-Goldwyn-Mayer to write a novel to be the basis for a feature film exploring the nature of America. The scheme involved four stories: one about the Pilgrims settling the New World; one about the confusion and conflict faced by Americans during the Revolutionary War; one about the generation that settled the West and lived through the Civil War; and a framing action beginning and ending the novel in the last years of World War II. Sandburg expected to complete the novel in less than a year, but it grew to more than one thousand pages and was not published until October 1948. It was never made into a film.

The novel is not a family saga, and no plot thread unifies it, but the four stories are linked in other ways. A plaque inscribed with the thirteenth-century English philosopher Roger Bacon's four Stumbling Blocks to Truth passes from story to story through the novel. Each of the novel's four stories features a protagonist with brick-red hair and a face half peaceful and half angry. Each of these protagonists has the initials "O. W.," and all have similar-sounding names; there are close similarities in other characters' names as well. The stories depict the lives of ordinary people, although famous historical personages also appear briefly. The stories are told with a wealth of historical detail.

Remembrance Rock, a best-seller, received a mixed critical reception. Many critics found some episodes gripping, some passages poetic, and the novel as a whole a clear witness of Sandburg's love of his country. However, they also found the action disconnected and overly elaborate, the dialogue unrealistic, the minor characters too numerous, the main characters more allegorical than convincing, and the work as a whole not so much a piece of fiction as a sermon that went on too long.

Resources

The most important collection of Carl Sandburg materials and manuscripts is at the University of Illinois at Urbana/Champaign. Other collections may be found at the University of Virginia; the University of Texas at Austin; and Knox College in Sandburg's hometown of Galesburg, Illinois. Other sources of interest to students of Carl Sandburg include the following:

The Carl Sandburg Historic Site. The house in which Sandburg was born in Galesburg, Illinois, is supported by the state of Illinois and the nonprofit Carl Sandburg Historic Site Association. A visitor's center houses a museum, gift shop, and small theater that shows videos about Sandburg. (http://www.sandburg.org/)

The Carl Sandburg Home National Historic Site. The house Sandburg occupied during the last twenty-two years of his life, Connemara, in Flat Rock, North Carolina, is open to visitors. Tours of the house and grounds are available. (http://www.nps.gov/carl/)

Audio Recordings. Sandburg made many sound recordings. Phonograph records were issued on the Caedmon, Columbia, and Decca labels, among others. They include recitals in which Sandburg reads from his works and performances in which he sings folk songs. Recordings available on cassette include *Carl Sandburg Reads* and Aaron Copland's *Lincoln Portrait*, narrated by Carl Sandburg.

World Wide Web. Sites devoted to Sandburg include "Carl Sandburg: Chicago Poems" (http://www.carl-sandburg.com), which offers poems, a short biography, and a discussion group. The Academy of American Poets' "Poetry Exhibits: Carl Sandburg" (http://www.poets.org/poets/poets.cfm?prmID=29) is a comprehensive site with links to other sites. "Carl Sandburg Web" (http://alexia.lis.uiuc.edu/~rmrober/sandburg/home.htm) has a biography, frequently asked questions about Sandburg, and links.

DAVID W. COLE

Jack Warner Schaefer

BORN: November 19, 1907, Cleveland, Ohio
DIED: January 24, 1991, Santa Fe, New Mexico
IDENTIFICATION: Mid-twentieth-century writer of western fiction that
helped to popularize and later eulogize the Old West.

Jack Warner Schaefer's first novel, *Shane* (1949), became his most popular
and most critically praised novel and continues to be widely read. Although
he wrote other novels that exceeded the quality of *Shane* both in craftsmanship and in thematic substance, only *Shane* has gained the status of a classic.
Its mysterious, archetypal hero continues to evoke awe, fear, and love through
his consummate skill with a gun, his heart's longing for peace, and his inspiring capacity for honor, loyalty, courage, and sacrifice. The book has been
translated into more than thirty languages and has been used as a student text
in many high schools and colleges.

The Writer's Life

Jack Warner Schaefer was born on November 19, 1907, on Cleveland's East Side. He was the second of four children, two sons and two daughters, born to Carl Walter Schaefer and Minnie Luella Hively Schaefer.

Schaefer's father was a lawyer, an enthusiastic expert on Abraham Lincoln, a lover of frontier history, and a personal friend of Carl Sandburg. Schaefer's own love for the West and for the beauty of words was surely nurtured in his home environment, where both parents were avid readers.

Childhood. When Schaefer was three, the family moved from Cleveland's East Side to nearby Lakewood. There he enjoyed a contented childhood in a large, new family home, where his love for literature and music was both encouraged and rewarded. In high school, he played piano, played in the school band, participated in the student council, and was a member of the debate club, the Spanish club, Hi-Y, the track team, and the National Honor Society.

Not surprisingly, Schaefer developed a love for books at an early age. He enjoyed reading almost anything, but he particularly enjoyed the Tarzan stories and the historical adventure novels of Alexandre Dumas. His yen for writing became more obvious in high school, where he wrote for and edited *The Arrow*, the school's literary magazine, and became editor of the yearbook, *The Cinema*.

College Years. After graduating from Lakewood High School in 1925, Schaefer continued his interest in creative writing at Oberlin College, where he majored in English, with a special concentration in Greek and Latin clas-

Schaefer (bottom row, far left) along with other staff members of *The Shaft,* the literary magazine at Oberlin College. On the top row to the left is Shaefer's sister Dorothy, who was the editor of the magazine. Their other two siblings attended Oberlin as well.

sics. He published frequently in the literary magazine *The Shaft* and eventually became its editor. His writings indicate that he admired the work of, among others, Daniel Defoe, Edwin Arlington Robinson, and Robinson Jeffers. He earned a bachelor of arts degree in 1929 and then went on to graduate study at Columbia University, where he specialized in eighteenth-century literature. However, his proposal to write a thesis on the history of motion pictures was rejected as unliterary. Such a restricted view of academic scholarship disgusted Schaefer, and he left Columbia at the end of his first year.

Journalism and Domestic Life.
Disillusioned with academia, Schaefer turned to journalism. He joined the news service of United Press in New Haven, Connecticut, as a rewrite man. For the next twenty years he honed his writing skills, especially as an editorial writer for various newspapers in Connecticut, Maryland, and Virginia. He deliberately cultivated a concise and concrete writing style and insisted that editorial convictions be founded on thorough research and sound reasoning.

On August 26, 1931, Schaefer married Eugenia Hammond Ives. They had four children: Carl, Christopher, Emily, and Jonathan. After seventeen years, the marriage ended in divorce. Schaefer married his second wife, Louise Wilhide Deans, in June 1949, acquiring three stepdaughters in the process: Sharon, Stephani, and Claudia.

The Turning Point.
Like his father, Schaefer had a lively interest in American history, particularly the history of the West. He began writing stories while manning the late-night desk of the *Norfolk Virginian-Pilot*. One story about a legendary but conflicted western hero grew to novel length. Schaefer submitted it to *Argosy* in 1946. There, through incredible luck, an editor picked up the manuscript by

Scheafer at Oberlin around 1929, every inch the gentleman. He stands in stark contrast to the black-clad villains that would populate some of his fiction.

mistake, read it, and accepted it for publication as a three-part serial under the title *Rider from Nowhere*. Subsequently, Schaefer revised the story and submitted it for publication as a novel, which was published as *Shane* by Houghton Mifflin in 1949. Schaefer's first novel, a popular and critical success from the start, soon terminated his profession in journalism and launched his new career as a novelist and short-story writer.

Schaefer now turned earnestly to the craft of short-story writing. During the next four years he published two volumes of short stories and completed three novels, all of them about an American West he had never personally seen. However, in 1955 *Holiday* magazine sent him on assignment to the West for a series of articles, and he felt truly at home there. Shortly after his return east, he and his wife packed up their belongings, drove to New Mexico, built a ranch close to Santa Fe, and settled in.

A New Direction. When he began to realize that the development and civilization of the West was destroying it, Schaefer grew disenchanted and ceased writing fiction. After completing his last novel, *Mavericks*, in 1967, he turned to writing nonfiction works such as *An American Bestiary* (1975) and *Conversations with a Pocket Gopher and Other Outspoken Neighbors* (1978), in which his animal narrators indict the human species for its failure to take proper care of the earth. The books reflect Schaefer's own growing bitterness about human blindness to the needs of the natural world.

Last Years. Unlike some writers, Schaefer did not continue writing until his death. During his long career, he published twenty books, which include nine novels, a number of which have been adapted as films. Schaefer took pleasure in being honored with an honorary doctorate in literature from his alma mater in 1989. In general, however, he felt that he had been unjustly dismissed as a "mere Western writer" and that, by popularizing the American West, he had contributed to its demise. Schaefer died of congestive heart failure on January 24, 1991, in Santa Fe.

Oberlin College as it appeared around the time Schaefer attended. It was one of his greatest thrills to return to the campus in 1989 and receive an honorary doctorate from the school.

HIGHLIGHTS IN SCHAEFER'S LIFE

1907   Jack Warner Schaefer is born on November 19 in Cleveland, Ohio.

1925   Graduates from Lakewood High School; enters Oberlin College.

1929   Graduates from Oberlin with a bachelor's degree in English and the classics.

1929   Pursues graduate study at Columbia University.

1930   Begins work as reporter for United Press in New Haven, Connecticut.

1931   Marries Eugenia Hammond Ives.

1931   Serves for seven years as assistant director of education for the Connecticut State Reformatory.

1932   Serves as associate editor of the *New Haven Journal-Courier*.

1939   Is promoted to position of editor at *New Haven Journal-Courier*.

1942   Moves to the *Baltimore Sun* as editorial writer.

1944   Moves to the *Norfolk Virginian-Pilot* as associate editor.

1948   Divorces Eugenia Ives.

1949   Marries Louise Wilhide Deans; becomes editor of the *Shoreliner* in New Haven; does freelance writing; publishes his first novel, *Shane*.

1955   Is sent on assignment to the West by *Holiday* magazine; shortly after his return, he moves his family to Santa Fe, New Mexico.

1960   Publishes *Old Ramon*, which is named the *New York Herald Tribune*'s Spring Book Festival Honor Book.

1961   *Old Ramon* is distinguished as a Newbery Honor Book and receives the Ohioana Award.

1962   Schaefer receives the Aurianne Award for *Old Ramon*.

1975   Receives the Distinguished Achievement Award from the Western Literature Association.

1985   Receives the Golden Spur Award for best western novel ever written.

1986   Receives the Levi-Strauss Saddleman Award for *Shane*.

1989   Receives an honorary doctorate in literature from Oberlin.

1991   Dies of congestive heart failure in Santa Fe, New Mexico, on January 24.

SHANE   Jack Schaefer
The Critical Edition   Edited by James C. Work

The Writer's Work

Jack Warner Schaefer wrote novels, short stories, a screenplay, and nonfiction. Most of his writing reflects his knowledge of and interest in the West; his admiration for individual courage, character, and endurance; and his artistic ability to write with depth and passion and stylistic finesse. He intended to prove that western literature need not be a lesser genre. He succeeded in doing so; however, his quintessential Western novel, *Shane,* is the one for which he is remembered, and the one that continues to be read.

Issues in Schaefer's Fiction. Early on, Schaefer felt sympathy for the culture of the West. In *Shane*, he clearly pulls for the fledgling community of pioneer farmers pitted against the cattle barons intent on controlling the wide open range. Schaefer felt that the time had come for self-seeking, rampant individualism to give way to the needs and interests of community; moreover, he was optimistic about the human capacity to establish a just society.

Eventually, however, Schaefer became disillusioned with the American culture that produced men whose notion of civilization was not only to tame the environment but also to destroy it if it stood in the way of their notion of progress. Thus, industry and technology came to dominate nature. Urban sprawl began to destroy the land and to ruin the beauty of the environment. Schaefer's last novel, *Mavericks*, mirrors this philosophical reversal: The law of the land is now the villain and the individual the victim.

People in Schaefer's Fiction. Because Schaefer wrote about such a range of settings, actions, and experiences, his characters also constitute a motley assembly that includes gunslingers, shepherds, rustlers, homesteaders, and Native Americans. Most live ordinary lives in search of meaning. Some reflect the innocent ideals of western expansion, dreaming of a peaceful place in community. Others represent the shattered innocence of the sullied frontier, where industrialization and greedy capitalism turned dreams into nightmares.

Accordingly, one type of Schaefer hero engages in physical and moral action that inspires admiration. Among the most memorable of such heroes is Shane, who longs for a place to settle down but is forced into violence when the lives of the innocent and the well-being of a community are threatened. He consequently faces exile. Other such heroes are Old Ramon, the simple shepherd; Little Bear in *The Canyon*

The livelihood of homesteaders is threatened in this scene from the 1953 film version of *Shane*. Some families who had moved west in search of opportunity came into conflict with the land-hungry cattle barons intent on control. Schaefer's novel centers on this irony-the West, a sprawling symbol of freedom and individuality, becomes a place of restriction and the need to conform.

(1953); and Jared Heath in *Company of Cowards* (1957). All are men of principle who, sometimes against great odds, rise to a high level of integrity and nobility.

A second type of Schaefer hero exhibits the same quality of steadfast purpose but evokes sympathy in defeat. Such heroes are portrayed in *The Kean Land and Other Stories* (1959), *Monte Walsh* (1963), and *Mavericks*; these protagonists are victimized by their culture's notion of progress, effectively destroying their way of life.

Schaefer's life in the West and his habit of thorough research enabled him to create vivid and authentic characters. All of Schaefer's heroes, successful or unsuccessful, are virtuously true to themselves.

The Theme of Self-Knowledge. The injunction to "know thyself" is an ancient one, but it is strongly present in Schaefer's fiction. Self-knowledge comes most often at the end of a process of growing up, of becoming aware of the world and how one fits or does not fit into it, of being tested and tried and learning about bravery and wisdom. In Schaefer's work, the characters who gain self-knowledge accept their essential natures and act accordingly. As Shane tells Bob Starrett just before he must leave all that he has come to love, "A man is what he is."

Some sadness invariably accompanies the growth toward self-knowledge. Shane's destiny excludes a peaceful family life. The young boy in *Old Ramon* must accept the loss of his beloved dog. Little Bear in *The Canyon* must embrace the community that expects conformity. Jared Heath in *Company of Cowards* suffers shame and disgrace before he finds redemption, and Jake Hanlon in *Mavericks* hangs on to his hard-bitten integrity even though his way of life and his values have been rejected and destroyed by progress. In Schaefer's work, to know oneself is also to be true to oneself.

Schaefer's Literary Legacy. *Shane* is well known around the world, having been translated into more than thirty languages. It

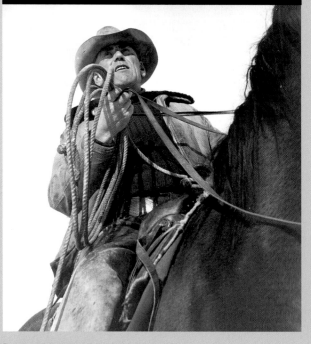

FILMS BASED ON SCHAEFER'S STORIES

1953   *Shane*

1953   *The Silver Whip*

1956   *Tribute to a Bad Man*

1957   *Trooper Hook*

1964   *Advance to the Rear*

1966   *Shane* (TV)

1967   *Stubby Pringle's Christmas* (TV)

1970   *Monte Walsh*

Some critics see the character of Shane, embodied here in this image of a cowboy around 1950, as the ultimate portrayal of the western hero haunted by his past. Shane is a brooding loner, the tragic figure whose sense of duty ensures he must sacrifice his own best interests so the community can endure.

has been praised as the best Western novel ever written. General readers appreciate its good-versus-evil conflict, its taut suspense, and especially its mysterious hero. Literary critics admire its stylistic finesse, depth of characterization, and universality of theme. This book alone ensures Schaefer's literary legacy.

Should Schaefer's other works be rediscovered, his legacy would be significantly enhanced. Schaefer wrote a body of literature that demonstrates his artistic virtuosity as well as his humanizing sympathy for the fringe members of society. Moreover, Schaefer is a superb historical chronicler of the American frontier—of both its innocence and its demise.

BIBLIOGRAPHY

Erisman, Fred. "Growing Up with the American West: Fiction of Jack Schaefer." In *The Popular Western*, edited by Richard W. Etulain and Michael T. Marsden. Bowling Green, Ohio: Bowling Green University Popular Press, 1974.

_____. "Jack Schaefer." In *A Literary History of the American West*, edited by J. Golden Taylor. Fort Worth: Texas Christian University Press, 1987.

Haslam, Gerald. *Jack Schaefer*. Boise, Idaho: Boise State University Press, 1975.

Mikkelsen, Robert. "The Western Writer: Jack Schaefer's Use of the Western Frontier." In *Shane: The Critical Edition*, edited by James C. Work. Lincoln: University of Nebraska Press, 1984.

Newer, Henry. "An Interview with Jack Schaefer." In *Shane: The Critical Edition*, edited by James C. Work. Lincoln: University of Nebraska Press, 1984.

Smith, C. E. J., ed. *Jack Schaefer and the American West*. London: Longman, 1978.

Torres, Louis. "Jack Schaefer: Teller of Tales." *Aristos*, October-December, 1996.

SOME INSPIRATIONS BEHIND SCHAEFER'S WORK

Jack Warner Schaefer's love of language began in his childhood home, where his parents, as avid readers, were excellent models. His father's friendship with Carl Sandburg led Schaefer to an early enjoyment of Sandburg's biography *Abraham Lincoln: The Prairie Years* (1926). Schaefer read both popular fare and the classics and was especially impressed by the historical novels of the nineteenth-century French writer Alexandre Dumas, the elder.

Schaefer's extraordinary love for the beauty and power of language was also inspired by the craft of the short-story writer Wilbur Daniel Steele, with whom Schaefer became friends. Schaefer regarded Steele as the greatest of the short story masters.

Early on, however, Schaefer also developed a love for the Old West and the western novels of Zane Grey. It was this love that eventually drove him to follow his heart out West. Schaefer credited his college teachers for nurturing both his appreciation for literary craftsmanship and his interest in the history of the West. However, it was Schaefer's own ranch near Santa Fe, New Mexico, and his own life on the frontier that gave him the greatest sense of the place and the people that informed all his writing with authenticity and passion.

Like the novels of Jack Schaefer, Frederic Remington's oil painting *A Dash for the Timber* (Amon Carter Museum, Fort Worth, Texas) finds its inspiration in the romance of western lore.

Reader's Guide to Major Works

MONTE WALSH

Genre: Novel
Subgenre: Picaresque Western
Published: Boston, 1963
Time period: 1872–1913
Setting: New Mexico

Themes and Issues. As *Shane* embodies the righteous and heroic defender of a young country's progress toward settling and civilizing its frontier, *Monte Walsh* reveals how that progress has diminished the human spirit. The story chronicles the life of Monte Walsh from age sixteen in 1872 to his death in 1913. The narrative's time frame spans the years of the West's transition from an open range worked by fiercely independent, solitary cowboys to an increasingly technological society where the former cowboys become ranch hands for eastern-owned syndicates and money replaces character as the highest value. Although the novel's thematic threads emphasize common Jack Warner Schaefer themes of growing up, relationships, and self-knowledge, they also reflect Schaefer's clearly shifting feelings about the West.

The Plot. It has been clear since childhood that Monte Walsh has a special love for horses. At age sixteen he and his horse go in search of adventure. The cattle industry is flourishing, and Monte soon becomes a seasoned cowpoke. When he meets Chet Rollins in Dodge City one night, he forms a lifelong friendship. Both young men are footloose and fancy free, drifting around the Great Plains and eventually to New Mexico.

Monte Walsh chronicles one man's passive resistance to change. Slowly, cattle drives, such as this one in Dodge City, Kansas, were becoming a thing of the past. One reviewer notes the quiet tragedy in Monte Walsh's desire to hold onto "that brief but fascinating period in American history when the western lands were unfenced and cattle was king."

However, the times are changing: Ranges are turning into ranches, and scattered farm communities are becoming towns. Chet changes too; he gets married and enters the world of business and eventually politics. Monte does not change. As his world slowly passes, Monte becomes more and more of an anachronism. Former cowboys now string fence and tend sheep. Monte, like Huck Finn, repeatedly pushes on toward more remote frontier territory where freedom, grit, and self-reliance are still valued.

However, Monte's physical toughness becomes fatally weakened. In fighting a blaze, his lungs are seared and permanently damaged. The death of Monkey Face, his dun horse, strikes an even more cruel blow. Monte has lost his health, his best friend, and his horse. Still, he remains true to himself. His last act equals Shane's both in courage and in self-sacrifice. In a big storm, Monte leaves the shelter of a remote mine where he has been working and rides his horse out to fetch a doctor for an accident victim. It is his last victory, as he believes that "no automobile could've done it," but also his final defeat: His lungs fail, and he dies. Chet comes to bury Monte, inscribing on his tombstone, "A Good Man with a Horse."

Analysis. Originally published in sections of related stories and episodes, *Monte Walsh* became Schaefer's longest, most ambitious, and most critically acclaimed novel. It serves as an interesting counterpoint to *Shane*. In *Monte Walsh*, the cowboy is not depicted as bully or brute but as an individual of steely integrity who works hard and plays hard and accepts the consequences of his own actions. He is driven by a fiercely independent spirit and, regardless of change, remains true to himself and to a primitive but free frontier way of life. The world that no longer has a place for such men and discards their values as expired is a diminished, fenced-in world of uniformity and complacency.

The Hollywood film version of *Monte Walsh* (1969), starring Jack Palance and Lee Marvin, appropriately captures Schaefer's nostalgia as a requiem for a cowboy. However, it falls short of equaling the vitality and richness of his novel.

SOURCES FOR FURTHER STUDY

Cleary, Michael. "Jack Schaefer: The Evolution of Pessimism." *Western American Literature* 14 (Spring 1979): 33–47.

Work, James C., ed. *Shane: The Critical Edition*. Lincoln: University of Nebraska Press, 1984.

LONG FICTION

1949   Shane
1953   The Big Range
1953   First Blood
1953   The Canyon
1957   Company of Cowards
1960   Old Ramon
1963   Monte Walsh
1964   Stubby Pringle's
        Christmas
1967   Mavericks

SHORT FICTION

1953   The Big Range
1954   The Pioneers
1955   Out West: An Anthology
        of Stories

1959   The Kean Land and
        Other Stories
1966   The Collected Stories of
        Jack Schaefer

NONFICTION

1963   The Great Endurance
        Horse Race: Six
        Hundred Miles on a
        Single Mount, 1908,
        from Evanston,
        Wyoming, to Denver
1965   Heroes Without Glory:
        Some Good Men of the
        Old West
1966   Adolphe Francis
        Alphonse Bandelier

1967   New Mexico
1975   An American Bestiary
1978   Conversations with a
        Pocket Gopher and
        Other Outspoken
        Neighbors

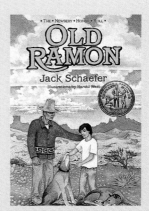

SHANE

Genre: Novel
Subgenre: Western
Published: Boston, 1949
Time period: 1889
Setting: Wyoming

Themes and Issues. The story of an adolescent's adulation and an adult's quest for a place and peace focuses on the universal theme of self-knowledge. Schaefer sets *Shane* in a Wyoming valley torn by conflicts between pioneer farmers and a resident cattle baron trying to retain the open range. Set in 1889, one year before the closing of the frontier, the novel mirrors the early U.S. historical conflict between rugged individualism and civilized community life. Schaefer wrote the story not only because he was fascinated with the American West but also because he wanted to prove that good literature could be created about the West as well as about the East or the South.

The Plot. The Starrett family lives in uneasy peace. Their hired hand has been run off by Fletcher, the unscrupulous open-range rancher who feels that his way of life is being threatened by the homesteaders. A mysterious figure named Shane comes riding into the valley and asks for a night's lodging. He soon endears himself to the family with his quiet strength and dignity and stays on to help Joe Starrett

In this still from the film adaptation of *Shane*, Joe Starrett, played by actor Van Heflin, is seated while Shane, the stronger of the two characters (played by Alan Ladd), assesses the scene from the background. Although Schaefer was ultimately pleased with the film version of Shane, he told the Oberlin College alumni magazine that the title character was supposed to be a "dark, deadly person." In an attempt to boost Alan Ladd's sagging career, the studio cast the clean-cut blond actor in the role of the mysterious gunfighter. According to John C. Tibbets and James M. Welsh in their book *Novels into Films*, "Alan Ladd is too much a gentleman, far more civilized than the edgy character in the novel seems to be."

run the farm. When Starrett and Shane manage through almost superhuman effort to dig out the ironwood stump that had always defied attempts at removal, they cement a relationship that will be superior to Fletcher's power.

Fletcher's future demands that Starrett fail as leader of the farm community encroaching on his territory. He discovers, however, that to deal with Starrett he must first deal with Shane. Shane soon proves himself a formidable opponent. Fletcher therefore hires Stark Wilson, a ruthless gunslinger who sends a message of intimidation when he kills a homesteader in a fast-draw duel.

However, the only truly intimidating character in the story is Shane. Fiercely loyal to Starrett and terrible in his strength, Shane disables Chris, sent by Fletcher to taunt and provoke Shane by breaking his arm. The real showdown comes in Grafton's saloon, where four of Fletcher's men attack Shane. Starrett joins Shane in the battle, and the numerous enemies are no match for that partnership. Shane's authority with his six-gun is absolute. He eliminates Fletcher's insidious force and even Fletcher himself, whom he spies lurking on the balcony. In the shootout, Shane ensures peace and safety for the community of homesteaders.

Young Bob Starrett has been an observer throughout, adopting Shane as his hero and developing an intense personal love for his idol. He sees Shane ride into the valley at the beginning, and he sees him ride out at the end, wounded, alone, and tragic in his self-exile. He tells the story in retrospect as an adult, and it is clear that in his admiration for Shane, he learned much about good and evil and the way he wished to shape his own life.

Analysis. In *Shane*, Schaefer clearly favors the community of farming families that try to cultivate the land, establish a social order based on law, and move from a tradition of ranch life to farm life, of lawless individualism to communal responsibility. Not only the Starretts but also Shane himself underscore this desire.

Emerging from a mysterious past, Shane longs for a place where he can feel a sense of belonging, where he can cultivate not only the land but also a new self-identity based on peace, tranquillity, and relationship.

Shane's tragedy is, however, that his renown and unparalleled skill as fighter and gunslinger make it possible to enforce this transition for others but not for himself. He's a victim of his past and of his superb expertise. He would embrace nonviolence, but violence is needed to protect the rights of the community. He wants to belong to that community, but his role as enforcer of the right condemns him to the lonely plight of the exile. As he tells young Bob at the end, in the final analysis, "a man is what he is, and there's no breaking the mold."

Readers of all ages and many places and cultures have responded warmly to Schaefer's first novel. Still widely read, *Shane* links readers to Bob's point of view; he sees his hero as a man of great dignity, courage, strength, self-sacrifice, and sadness who did "what had to be done." Schaefer's literary craftsmanship in style, use of symbol, and classical form raises it well above the typical Western, as many critics have noted, and makes it deserving of its selection by a committee of British readers as one of the hundred best novels of the twentieth century. *Shane* also enjoyed success as a film when it came out in 1953, starring Alan Ladd and earning five Academy Award nominations and more than eight million dollars.

SOURCES FOR FURTHER STUDY

Folsom, James K. "*Shane* and *Hud*: Two Stories in Search of a Medium." *Western Humanities Review* 24 (Autumn 1970): 359–372.

Quinones, Ricardo J. *The Changes of Cain: Violence and the Lost Brother*. Princeton, N.J.: Princeton University Press, 1991.

Torres, Louis. "Jack Schaefer, Teller of Tales." *Aristos*, October-December, 1996.

Work, James C. "Settlement Waves and Coordinate Forces in *Shane*." *Western American Literature* 14 (Fall 1979): 191–200.

_____, ed. *Shane: The Critical Edition*. Lincoln: University of Nebraska Press, 1984.

Other Works

THE CANYON (1953). After *Shane*'s smashing success, Jack Warner Schaefer wanted to make sure that he would not be tempted by his sudden popularity to repeat himself over and over again. He wrote this book to please himself and always had a special fondness for it. It tells the story of a young man separating himself from his community in order to find himself and to live in harmony with his convictions.

Little Bear has a problem: He is a Cheyenne warrior who believes that it is wrong to fight, thus opposing the very basis of his people's culture. He exiles himself, falls into a canyon, suffers a broken leg, and manages to survive through courage and ingenuity. Finally a badger shows him how to find his way out of the canyon. Little Bear returns to his people in search of a wife to share an isolated canyon life with him.

After accomplishing an extraordinary feat of courage and service to his tribe, he is allowed to marry Spotted Turtle. They live peacefully but alone in the canyon. Their first child is sickly and, without needed help and medicine, soon dies. Little Bear now realizes that no one is an island and that people need each other. Thus, the two return to their community. The protagonist's quest for spiritual wholeness proves complex, and its fulfillment in a society of conflicting values is not easily accomplished.

COMPANY OF COWARDS (1957). Jared Heath is an officer in the Civil War. During one deadly and confusing battle, he walks away from the front line, escaping certain death. He is subsequently accused of cowardice and stripped of his rank and command. His family, of a proud military background, is humiliated and disowns him. Much worse is his own sense of failure. He accepts a chance to redeem himself by leading a small group of other busted officers and nonofficers to New Mexico. There, in a battle with American Indians, Heath proves his true leadership. Although his ragged group of fellow soldiers suffers from diverse mental and emotional scars that render them quite unfit for battle, Heath molds them into a unit of absolute loyalty. They follow their commander as he leads the charge, and heedless of their own safety, they become conquering heroes.

Schaefer makes it clear that the novel's main action is Jared Heath's journey into himself. The demon that pursues him is failure. Devastated by that discovery, Heath is not so much driven to repair his reputation as to recover the self he feels he has lost. When everyone's rank is restored after the heroic victory, Heath regains his self-respect and rides away with an "enduring quietness within."

MAVERICKS (1967). Schaefer wrote this novel as his epitaph, a lament of the passing of the Old West, destroyed by the changes of a relentlessly advancing civilization. Old Jake Hanlon, like Monte Walsh, is among the last of the traditional cowboys. His life, like the life of his herd of mustangs, has been rendered obsolete. All Jake can do now, before he dies, is replay the memories of his life in the saddle of his beloved horse, Jimmie Dunn.

He remembers how man and horse won a 530-mile race against all competition. He nostalgically remembers the mustangs he has owned and how he has tried to save their dwindling numbers from the pursuit of trucks and planes and indifferent syndicates that were eager to turn them into dog food.

What Jake remembers is a colorful time of vitality, physical skill, strength of will, and open camaraderie. That time has been lost. Now highways lead eastern profiteers into the Southwest, destroying a way of life that may have been characterized by primitive values but whose integrity was unquestionable. Now hollow men, their pockets lined with money, are in control, and they regard Jake Hanlon and men like him as disgraces to civilized community.

In all Jake's remembering, nothing is more painful than the realization that he himself has participated in the process of destruction. It is a sad conclusion to a long, hard life. It is also a sad conclusion to Schaefer's western novel writing, which began with such an optimistic vision in *Shane*. He saved some of his best writing for the last; many reviewers raved about this novel, calling *Mavericks* "a magnificent tribute to a vanishing breed of men and horses."

OLD RAMON (1960). One summer, an old sheepherder takes the young son of his patron along with him into the harsh and dangerous Mojave Desert in search of food and shelter for the flocks. The trip becomes the young boy's initiation into both the beauty and the terror of life. He learns about rattlesnakes and wolves, about storms and stampedes, and about losing what one loves, when a wolf kills his beloved sheepdog. Through the firm tutelage of the aging shepherd, the boy also learns about survival, courage, and friendship. Above all, he learns that maturity requires one to temper bravery with wisdom. This Newbery Honor Book is written with a quiet, moving power and is equally enjoyable for young and older readers.

Resources

The American Heritage Center, at the University of Wyoming in Laramie, houses a substantial collection of Jack Warner Schaefer's papers, including manuscripts of his published and unpublished fiction as well as foreign editions of his fiction. Oberlin College's library holds more than two hundred of Schaefer's own works, books for which he wrote introductions, and secondary sources. The Oberlin College Archives contain a collection of Schaefer's correspondence and copies of the student magazine he edited. Other sources of interest for students of Jack Schaefer include the following:

Jack Schaefer Home Page. This Web site includes background information on the author and his works, features an extensive bibliography, and gives information on the Schaefer archives. An online journal, *Schaefer Studies*, is also available. (http://www.aristos. org/schaefer/htm)

Audiocassettes. *Shane* (1992) and *The Canyon* are both available in recorded versions. *Shane* is read by Dick Cavett.

HENRY J. BARON

Anne Sexton

BORN: November 9, 1928, Newton, Massachusetts
DIED: October 4, 1974, Weston, Massachusetts
IDENTIFICATION: New England poet of the 1960s and 1970s known for her powerful poems of mental illness and collapse.

An important member of the group of self-revealing "confessional" poets, Anne Sexton wrote poetry about her struggle with depression and her suicide attempts. Revealing intimate aspects of her life as a woman struggling to gain consciousness, she experimented with new lyrical forms, pioneering the confessional mode. Her work is often graphic and shocking, but its power lies partly in her ability to make myths out of her own experiences. She identified with characters from folktales and fairy tales, weaving her story into theirs. Her poems remain powerful because she invoked the archetypes of myth and legend while narrating the most painful episodes in her life.

The Writer's Life

Anne Gray Harvey was born in Newton, Massachusetts, in 1928. Although she reached great heights of success, Anne Sexton was never comfortable with herself. The roots of her insecurity reach back to her early years. Her father ran a successful wool concern in Massachusetts, and the family was well-off financially. However, Sexton had an uncomfortable family life in the emotional sense and consistently felt unwanted and unloved.

Childhood. Sexton wrote poems as a child, but when two were published in her high school yearbook, her mother accused her of plagiarism—which made her stop writing for a

long time. Feeling rejected by her parents, especially her mother, she chose a great aunt, Anna Ladd Dingley, as a surrogate mother figure. Her great aunt went insane in old age and had to be hospitalized. Sexton kept getting into trouble in both public and private school, and it was suggested to her parents that she be taken to a psychiatrist, but this was not done.

Young Womanhood. After an unwanted year at Garland Junior College, more of a finishing school for women than a real college, she eloped with her boyfriend, Alfred Muller Sexton II, nicknamed "Kayo." In 1948 at the age of nineteen, she tried to leave her past be-

The young newlyweds embark on their twenty-five-year marriage. It was a tumultuous union, which was able to withstand Anne's frequent infidelities. Kayo willingly stayed in the background in the wake of his wife's mounting fame and success as a writer.

Sexton flanked by her daughters, Joyce and Linda. Beneath the smile, strain and depression were becoming an ever-present theme. Poetry became an outlet as she struggled with her roles as wife and mother.

hind. The newly married Anne Sexton went to modeling school and worked as a model—pictures from this period show a glamorous and self-possessed young woman. She played the role of the young wife, learning to economize because she no longer had access to family money. When the Korean War began in 1950, Kayo joined the U.S. Navy and was shipped overseas, thus leaving Anne on her own for some time.

Anne gave birth to her first daughter, Linda, in 1953. Afterward she suffered from such serious depression that she began to visit an analyst—which she would do off and on for the rest of her life. The birth of her second daughter, Joyce ("Joy"), was followed by a severe nervous breakdown, which ended in a suicide attempt. Her therapist told her that writing poetry would be therapeutic, so Sexton began to write. A creative-writing seminar conducted by John Holmes brought her into contact with the poet Maxine Kumin, and the two women became fast friends.

Sexton's abilities developed rapidly. Enrolled in Robert Lowell's writing class at Boston University, she met Sylvia Plath, another troubled poet with a suicide obsession. Sexton and Plath became friendly and discussed the new kind of poetry they were writing. Sexton's first book, *To Bedlam and Part Way Back* (1960), told the story of her mental breakdown and her vigorous attempt at recovery. Her second book, *All My Pretty Ones* (1962), dealt with mental problems as well, but it also described her reactions to the deaths of her parents and other family members, which had left her feeling even more insecure.

Professional Life. Sexton's work caused a great stir in the literary world. Her kind of candid, revealing poetry, called "confessional" by critics, was also being written by others, in-

The poet Robert Lowell guided Sexton's budding talent. A crop of important new poets was emerging from his now legendary classes at Boston University in the late 1950s.

Sexton was eager to link poetry with other arts, making it into performance material suitable for a wider audience than poetry readers. Her autobiographical play, *45 Mercy Street*, was produced in 1969. She worked with various groups to create and stage musical adaptations of her works, which used various kinds of music and were designed to appeal to differing audiences.

Personal Life. Sexton's personal life did not mirror her public life; she spent her entire adulthood in therapy dealing with mental instability. Her relationship with her husband deteriorated and she had affairs with fellow poets, although she did not divorce until almost the end of her life. She had a difficult time playing the mother role, no doubt because she had never felt nurtured by her own mother. At one time she sent her daughter to live with her husband's parents, feeling too overwhelmed to care for her. Sexton was always hurt by negative criticism; although her work was bold, direct, and daring, she wanted it to be accepted. She attempted suicide several times, expressing anger over poet Sylvia Plath's suicide in 1963 and the fact that she had discussed suicide with Plath, who had now done it, and, in a sense, had "won" the suicide competition.

Sexton was made a full professor at Boston University in 1972, and although her life was full of teaching and presentations, she still suffered from severe depression that required periodic hospitalizations. Against her husband's will, she filed for a divorce in 1973, which was granted in November of that year. In 1974 Sexton's depression grew worse, although she frequently taught and traveled to give readings; she was also preparing a new book for publication. On October 4, the day after a reading at Goucher College, she had lunch with her long-time friend and collaborator, Maxine Kumin, came home, and finally committed suicide by carbon monoxide poisoning in the locked garage of her home.

cluding the popular poets Sylvia Plath, W. D. Snodgrass, and Robert Lowell, who is credited with founding the confessional school with the publication of his *Life Studies* (1959). Sexton became a highly sought-after speaker and teacher. Ironically, the woman who had completed only one year of junior college was a great academic success. She was granted the Crashaw Chair in Literature at Colgate University, membership in Phi Beta Kappa, and honorary doctorates from several prestigious schools. She was awarded a Guggenheim Fellowship and many other grants and prizes, including the 1967 Pulitzer Prize for poetry. At the time of her death she held a professorship at Boston University—no small achievement for someone who had run away from junior college to marry.

HIGHLIGHTS IN SEXTON'S LIFE

1928   Anne Gray Harvey is born on November 9 in Newton, Massachusetts.

1947–1948   Attends Garland Junior College in Boston, Massachusetts.

1948   Elopes with Alfred Muller "Kayo" Sexton II.

1949   Completes modeling course.

1951   Models for Hart Agency; Kayo enters Navy.

1953   Sexton's first daughter, Linda Gray, is born.

1954   Sexton undergoes therapy for depression.

1955   Second daughter, Joyce Ladd, is born.

1956   Sexton is encouraged by her psychiatrist to write after first psychiatric hospitalization and suicide attempt.

1957   Enrolls in John Holmes's poetry workshop; meets Maxine Kumin.

1959   Mother and father both die of illness.

1960   Sexton publishes first book of poetry, *To Bedlam and Part Way Back*.

1962   Publishes second book, *All My Pretty Ones*.

1963   Collaborates with Kumin on children's books; tours Europe on travel fellowship and Ford Foundation grant.

1966   Publishes *Live or Die*; goes on African safari.

1967   Receives Pulitzer Prize for *Live or Die*.

1968   Forms rock group, Anne Sexton and Her Kind; is awarded honorary Phi Beta Kappa by Harvard.

1969   Receives Guggenheim Fellowship; writes play *45 Mercy Street*, which is performed; begins teaching at Boston University.

1971   Publishes *Transformations*.

1972   Sexton is made full professor at Boston University; holds Crashaw Chair in Literature at Colgate University.

1973   Undergoes hospitalizations; is divorced from Kayo.

1974   Publishes *The Death Notebooks*; commits suicide October 4.

1981   *The Complete Poems* is published posthumously.

The Writer's Work

Anne Sexton is known for her poetry, although she also wrote a play and coauthored a number of children's stories. Her poetry is about her struggle for sanity and about the conflict between breakdown and desire for death on one hand and the love of life and the need for healing on the other.

Issues in Sexton's Poetry.

Even in her earliest work, Sexton describes the fight for healing, with feelings of depression and despair at war with a desire for health and stability. The main subjects in her poems are the ways in which despair can be fought. The metaphorical black pit is a constant in her work as it was in her life. In Sexton's life, none of her many honors, awards, publications, or family and friends was able to lift her from that pit. In her poetry, none of the methods of dealing with despair finally shows a clear solution. The struggle in her life that is so evident in her work makes her poetry powerful reading. Sexton used poetry as a therapeutic tool to keep her mental illness at bay; if the therapy did not cure her, it did provide much support.

Religion.
Sexton was interested in religion, and she used many images from Christianity in her work as she entertained the idea of joining a church. Catholicism in particular intrigued her, and she often used imagery from the Roman Catholic Church in her poetry. The term *confessional poet* has a special meaning when applied to Sexton, for she seemed to think of poetry as a priest's confessional, in which she could confess her sins and seemingly receive some kind of forgiveness. "I was born/ doing reference work in sin and born/ confessing it," she says in "With Mercy for the Greedy." Earlier in the poem, she thinks of the wooden cross that a friend has sent her, which she keeps and values but cannot totally accept, because "need is not quite belief." Although Sexton recognized the comfort that religion could provide, she was not able to accept it for herself. Many of her poems describe a need to know God, as well as the difficulty of doing so. The title *The Awful Rowing Toward God* communicates a sense of her struggle and her goal.

Mythology and Folklore.
Sexton came of age in a time when personal and professional options for women were more narrow and unappealing and conformity was highly valued. She was not, for instance, sent to a university,

A popular figure with a well-forged public persona, Sexton's often sensational subjects and dramatic flair lent her readings wide appeal. They were heavily attended, and her roster of appearances grew. She loved the acclaim, yet found the experiences harrowing each time, often taking a combination of prescription drugs before mounting the stage. Here Sexton is seen at one of her many social gatherings in 1968.

but rather to a college that was really a finishing school. In the traditional myths about women, and in legend and folklore, the happy ending is always a wedding. Perhaps Sexton was disappointed that the unhappiness of her childhood did not disappear when she eloped with Kayo. One of her major desires in poetry was to unmake myth, to tell women's stories realistically and yet within the framework of folklore. Sexton retells stories of women who come through trials to happy endings, but the endings of her stories are different—women's stories end in boredom, sadness, or horror, or even a combination of these. Her more difficult poems from the collection *Transformations* focus on these tales, and by their twists show how the stories traditionally told to young women are dangerous or untrue.

The Pull of Death. Sexton's mental illness always drew her toward suicide, and she wrote a number of poems about her fascination and flirtation with death. She wrote poems about taking sleeping pills given her in the hospital to fall asleep, a process she saw as a mini-death, and about her suicidal wishes and plans. She seems to be attempting to explain to an ordinary person how it is possible for one to spend so much of one's life wrestling with ideas about how to end it. In "Wanting to Die," she says,

Vincent Van Gogh's 1889 painting *Starry Night*. The swirls and eddies of the painter's vision provide the springboard for Sexton's poem of the same title, in which she considers her own mortality. "The town is silent," she writes. "The night boils with eleven stars/ Oh starry night! This is how/ I want to die."

"But suicides have a special language./ Like carpenters they want to know *which tools./* They never ask *why build.*"

Sexton identified with other suicidal artists, including the nineteenth-century Dutch expressionist painter Vincent Van Gogh. In one poem she describes his famous painting *Starry Night* (1889), in which brilliant, apparently swirling stars pull the reader's attention away from the dark blue sky and the black landscape; she saw the anguish suggested in the painting as pointing toward both God and her desired death.

Women's Lives. The many roles of women—mother, wife, daughter, individual—are present in all the poems, and may be the reason for Sexton's continued audience. Sexton described her life as daughter and mother in terms of the lives of women in folklore, as well as directly. Her poems are full of women, witches and hags, maidens, stepmothers, teachers, dancers. In a time of limited choices for women, she invented and explored alternatives and tried to find a way for a woman to be herself despite society's expectations of her.

Sexton's Legacy. Eclipsed at first by that of Sylvia Plath—her fellow poet and friend who committed suicide first—Sexton's reputation was reevaluated in the 1980s, in part because of the variety in her work and her unusual and original exploration of myth. Sexton was ahead of her time in her attempt to marry poetry with other arts, an interest that links her to the performance poets of the 1980s and 1990s. Her combination of self-revelation and showmanship is unique.

BIBLIOGRAPHY

Bixler, Francis, ed. *Original Essays on the Poetry of Anne Sexton*. Conway: University of Central Arkansas Press, 1988.

Colburn, Steven E., ed. *Anne Sexton: Telling the Tale*. Ann Arbor: University of Michigan Press, 1988.

George, Diana Hume. *Oedipus Anne: The Poetry of Anne Sexton*. Champaign: University of Illinois Press, 1986.

———, ed. *Anne Sexton: Selected Criticism*. Urbana: University of Illinois Press, 1988.

Hall, Caroline King Barnard. *Anne Sexton*. Boston: Twayne Publishers, 1989.

McClatchy, J. D., ed. *Anne Sexton: The Artist and Her Critics*. Bloomington: Indiana University Pres, 1978.

Middlebrook, Diane Wood. *Anne Sexton: A Biography*. Boston: Houghton Mifflin, 1991.

Northouse, Cameron, and Thomas P. Walsh. *Sylvia Plath and Anne Sexton: A Reference Guide*. Boston: G. K. Hall, 1974.

Wagner-Martin, Linda, ed. *Critical Essays on Anne Sexton*. Boston: G. K. Hall, 1989.

Because they succumbed to a similar fate, the work of Sexton and Sylvia Plath, despite sharing only vague similarities, is often compared and examined, diminishing the merits of each. Both became quasiarchetypal figures, self-destructive and tormented women unable to transcend the demands of their sex and their art. In the process, their individuality became eclipsed.

Anne Sexton's Posthumously Published Books

When Anne Sexton committed suicide in 1974, she had been in the process of reading the final galley proofs of her poetry collection *The Awful Rowing Toward God,* which was about to be published. In fact, she reviewed the proofs with her poet friend Maxine Kumin on the day she killed herself. This powerful collection was released shortly after her death and tells of her attempts to find and gain healing from God.

Sexton had still another manuscript in preparation at the time of her death, which she called *45 Mercy Street* (1976). This book, which she had partly edited, was prepared for publication by her daughter Linda Gray Sexton. In addition to this book, the poet left notebooks full of new poems, which her daughter edited and published as *Words for Dr. Y: Uncollected Poems with Three Stories* (1978). A few last poems included in neither of these books were added to *The Complete Poems,* published in 1981.

These two collections and the final poems add to the picture of Sexton that emerges from her other work. The last poems often lack the craft of her earlier work, although some of them had been revised or had been saved from earlier times. Some of these poems are desperate pleas from a woman who is no longer in control of her life. She goes over the deepest wounds of her life, trying to find some way to mend them. She addresses people from her childhood, trying to call them back and change the relationships that had existed between herself and them.

Mercy and Death. This volume is an attempt at healing, beginning with a poem that searches for "Mercy Street." Mercy represents relief and comfort for Sexton, a way out of her madness and misery. Although earlier collections found some relief in analysis, poetry, medication, and feminist myth, this one does not. If the poems do not end with the search still underway, they tend to end in despair. An especially effective poem, "Red Roses," tells of child abuse—the red roses are the bruises the three-year-old boy gets from his abusive mother, who dances him around and throws him against the wall to the tune of "Red Roses for a Blue Lady." In the hospital, he does not tell where his bruises came from, because he loves the mother who batters him. The poem makes no claims about the future of the two, but it seems that the abuse can end only in the child's death.

Although of interest to critics and scholars, the release of work left unpublished during a writer's lifetime often does little to improve his or her reputation. With Sexton, however, some readers believe her posthumous volumes embellish and complete the extended *cri de coeur* that marks her oeuvre.

Death dominates in "Bestiary U.S.A.," which begins with the poet's claim that she is looking at "the strangeness in them [the beasts] and the naturalness they cannot help, in order to find some virtue in the beast in me." What she finds, however, does not redeem her, although the poems have a grim charm. In the medieval bestiaries, each beast represented a human characteristic, usually a sin or virtue that the animal called to mind. In Sexton's naming of the animals, she uses vivid and memorable details to make them real. The animals nevertheless all suggest death; either they are dead when she describes them, or their aspect makes them symbols of death.

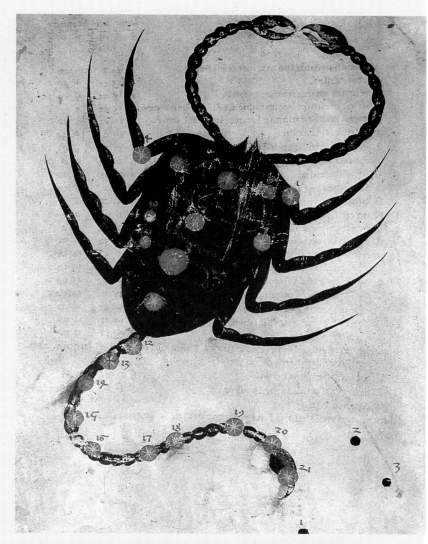

Scorpio or Scorpion, Signs of the Zodiac by an unknown artist. Series or sequences such as "Scorpio, Bad Spider, Die" underscore the vibrancy and formal innovation that were among Sexton's unique contributions to modern American poetry.

Early Works. The other collection, *Words for Dr. Y,* contains some of Sexton's earlier poems, which she had put aside to be published later, and some of her last poems, which do not have any mark of her demanding editorship. Some of these are desperate, questing poems showing Sexton's loss of the final shreds of control. It is hard to believe that while she wrote these, she was teaching and giving readings, having affairs, and carrying on friendships.

Other poems in this collection show some of her earlier craft and her dark humor. "Scorpio, Bad Spider, Die" is a sequence of horoscope poems that

Sexton made art out of her anguish. Her confessional style emerged from a desire to explore and understand her mental illness as well as a need to broadcast and publicize her pain.

shows the playfulness toward death that surfaces in Sexton's earlier work. Most of the poems begin with a date followed by a bland quotation from a horoscope, which leads into a crackling, hair-raising interpretation or application of the horoscope. Some of them revert to the rhyme and rhythm of her earlier work, as does "May 30," which ends "Please God, we're all right here. Please leave us alone./ Don't send death in his fat red suit and his ho-ho baritone." Again, however, Sexton's ambivalence is clear: She asks God not to send Death, but she sees Death as Santa Claus. The Scorpio poems had been written earlier and set aside, perhaps because they did not seem to fit thematically into any earlier collection. Their grim humor sparkles.

Last Words. Sexton's very last poems, written in the last few months of her life and included in *The Complete Poems,* tend to be personal and obscure, final notes to people whose presence haunted her. However, one poem, "In Excelsis," about a trip with her analyst, describes a contemplated sea-death: " . . . I would drink the moon/ and my clothes would slip away,/ and I would sink into the great mother arms/ I never had. . . ." This dream-death would provide both nurturing and release. The apparent joy of the title—a Latin phrase that means something like "in the highest" and is usually used in praise of God—is only joy at the possibility of life's ending.

Sexton's posthumous poetry shows her slide toward despair. This poetry is for the truly serious student of Anne Sexton's work, as often the covering of art, which is so very much a part of her earlier work, has slipped off to reveal the incurable pain of her madness.

Reader's Guide to Major Works

ALL MY PRETTY ONES

Genre: Poetry
Subgenre: Confessional poetry
Published: New York, 1962
Time Period: 1950s and 1960s
Setting: Generalized suburban landscapes

Themes and Issues. Anne Sexton's first book created an eager readership, mostly of women who were pleased to see their concerns put so boldly into poems. Her second book carried on the themes of the first, but with an additional focus on religion. Sexton's lifelong search for God surfaces in these poems. They also explore the hole left in her life by her parents' deaths, which occurred in 1959, and by the death of her beloved aunt, who had spent her last years in an institution. Sexton experiments with form in these poems, many of which are in free verse. Again, many of the central characters are women, as in "Woman with Girdle," "The Housewife," and "For Eleanor Boylan Talking with God." The collection begins with poems of a highly formal structure and works toward more open poems and free verse.

The Poems. Sexton said that one of the poems that continued to please her the most at the end of her career was "The Truth the Dead Know," a sixteen-line formal poem that begins the collection. Other popular poems are the title poem, "All My Pretty Ones," and the reader-friendly "Woman with Girdle."

SOME INSPIRATIONS BEHIND SEXTON'S WORK

Sexton stopped writing in high school after her mother accused her of plagiarism. She became active again when her therapist suggested that she write. This suggestion, made in 1954, gave her the freedom and the motivation to return to poetry.

Sexton's participation in John Holmes's writing seminar opened the door to a new literary world and introduced her to Maxine Kumin, her later friend and collaborator, as well as a host of other writers who provided support and encouragement. Following this seminar she met other poets later designated confessional poets, and she gained support for her idea that poetry could be both art and therapy.

Sexton's troubled relationship with her parents and their lack of support showed in her writing, especially her earlier work. The poems that she wrote after her parents' deaths describe her struggle to deal with the loss of these important, if unsupportive, figures in her life. She attempted through her poetry to come to terms with their memories.

The births of Sexton's two daughters influenced her work dramatically. First, the experience of depression after the births led her to write, and second, the fact and the meaning of motherhood took a central place in her work.

Sexton read *Grimm's Fairy Tales* (1823–1826) as a child, and they were a major influence on her work. Their starkness and their clarity appealed to her, and their morals about the roles of women provided her with material to dissect in her poetry.

In Louis-Welden Hawkins's ca. 1895 painting *Madame Severine* (Musée d'Orsay, Paris), a woman sits surrounded by correspondence and the weight of words. The poet's family was not immune to the distortions of censorship and the suppression of truth. In taking stock of her life in the early 1960s, Sexton wrangled with the distant and unreachable images of her parents, shadowy figures that haunt her second collection.

"The Truth the Dead Know" is about the deaths of Sexton's parents, which took place within three months in 1959. Her mother died first, of cancer, and her father died of a heart attack three months later. The poet "refuses the stiff procession to the grave" and instead goes to Cape Cod with her lover-husband. The poem contrasts the actions of the living—"when we touch/ we enter touch entirely"—with the absolute stillness of the dead, who "lie without shoes/ in their stone boats." The poem suggests that the only way to respond to death is to live fully and experience fully. Images of life and death contrast neatly throughout the four four-line stanzas.

"All My Pretty Ones" describes the poet's clearing out of her parents' house after her father's death. The title comes from William Shakespeare's play *Macbeth* (1606). When Macbeth's opponent Macduff learns that his wife and children have been killed, he says, "All my pretty ones?/ Did you say all? O hell-kite! All?/ What! all my pretty chickens and their dam/ At one fell swoop?" Despite Sexton's problematic relationship with her parents, it was difficult to lose both of them within three months. This poem describes in graceful rhymed verse her going through the family photographs in her parents' home. The poet discards photos that had once meant something to her parents but mean nothing to her. She goes through her father's collection of clippings and her mother's diary, which indicates her father's alcoholism only with silences and excuses. Now her father is only a photograph and lives only in her memory. She concludes: "Whether you are pretty or not, I outlive you,/ bend down my strange face to yours and forgive you."

"Woman with Girdle" is an unusually high-spirited poem for Sexton; it simply describes a woman who is taking off her girdle. The woman pulls the casing down over her flabby body and finally stands there unbound, relieved, and fully herself. She rises "a city from the sea." This removal of bonds is a kind of rebirth: "straightway from God you have come/ into your redeeming skin." In a time of conformity and rigidity, a girdle—that staple of preparation for work that was nearly as common as makeup—made a good symbol for the constraints that were then placed on women. It is a false skin, required by the world; the true skin is suppressed beneath it and is "redeemed" by its release.

Analysis. The powerful emotional bluntness of these poems made Sexton an internationally known figure and earned her several awards. However, not all response was positive. Some critics felt that she bared too much. There were

POETRY

1960 To Bedlam and Part Way Back
1962 All My Pretty Ones
1964 Selected Poems
1966 Live or Die
1968 Poems (with Thomas Kinsella and Douglas Livingston)
1969 Love Poems
1971 Transformations
1972 The Book of Folly
1974 The Death Notebooks
1975 The Awful Rowing Toward God
1976 45 Mercy Street
1978 Words for Dr. Y: Uncollected Poems with Three Stories
1981 The Complete Poems
1988 Selected Poems of Anne Sexton

PLAYS

1969 45 Mercy Street

NONFICTION

1977 Anne Sexton: A Self-Portrait in Letters

1985 No Evil Star: Selected Essays, Interviews, and Prose

CHILDREN'S LITERATURE

1963 Eggs of Things (with Maxine Kumin)
1964 More Eggs of Things (with Kumin)
1971 Joey and the Birthday Present (with Kumin)
1975 The Wizard's Tears (with Kumin)

critics who believed that it was acceptable for men, but not for women, to discuss their drinking problems, mental breakdowns, and divorces. Sexton's second book affirmed the promise of her first—that she would gloss over nothing, that she would tell the truth as she saw it.

Fellow poet Louise Bogan commented, "These are almost always women's secrets that do not, in the ordinary way of things, get told. To outline personal relationships . . . always at a high pitch of emotion requires courage. . . ." After the publication of *All My Pretty Ones*, Sexton became a major force in the literary world; her readings were crowded and were frequently followed by debate.

SOURCES FOR FURTHER STUDY

Middlebrook, Diane Wood. *Anne Sexton: A Biography.* Boston: Houghton Mifflin, 1991.

Northouse, Cameron, and Thomas P. Walsh. *Sylvia Plath and Anne Sexton: A Reference Guide.* Boston: G. K. Hall, 1974.

Sexton, Linda Gray. *Searching for Mercy Street: My Journey Back to My Mother, Anne Sexton.* Boston: Little, Brown, 1994.

Wagner-Martin, Linda, ed. *Critical Essays on Anne Sexton.* Boston: G. K. Hall, 1989.

THE AWFUL ROWING TOWARD GOD

Genre: Poetry
Subgenre: Confessional poetry
Published: New York, 1975
Time period: Early 1970s
Setting: Generalized suburban landscapes

Themes and Issues. These poems are Sexton's attempt to cure her mental illness through religion—not organized religion, but an effort-filled personal contact with God. *The Awful Rowing Toward God* was published after her death; she read the galley proofs from the publisher on the day of her suicide. The free-verse, labored poems indicate her desire to be received and healed. The figures of her old nightmares are all there; she chases down the sources of her discomfort and identifies them, then she asserts her need to be healed and describes her efforts to find a god who will accept her. She explores elements of Christianity, particularly of Roman Catholicism, that might apply to her illness. This book is an organized description of a spiritual journey.

The Poems. The two poems that begin and end this book are particularly noteworthy; they are "Rowing" and "The Rowing Endeth." They frame the middle poems, which define Sexton's spiritual quest, in traditional but typically quirky Sexton terms.

"Rowing" begins with Sexton's own unhappy childhood: "I was stamped out like a Plymouth fender/ into this world./ First came the crib/ with its glacial bars . . . / Then there was life/ with its cruel houses . . . / but I grew,/ like a pig in a trenchcoat I grew. . . ." She thinks of God as "like an island I had not rowed to," and sets forth for this island. Her troubles and her mental illness she pictures as a "rat" and imagines a meeting between herself and God, where he will take the "gnawing pestilential rat" in his hands "and embrace it." She wants God not to kill the rat—her troubles and herself—but to embrace it, to make it stop gnawing her insides. She concludes, "The story ends with me still rowing." She actively seeks God's help, and it takes all her energy, as does rowing to a distant island.

It is worth noting that the rat is one of Sexton's most frequent images. She writes about rats from her first poems onward, the rat being that destructive and yet vital animal that she imagines dwelling inside her, removable only by God. She was fascinated by the statement "Rats live on no evil star" because it is a palindrome, a statement that reads the same right to left as left to right. She wrote a poem with this title and asked that the saying be carved on her tombstone.

The last poem of the collection, "The Rowing Endeth," sees her arriving on God's island and playing a game of poker with Him— a game He wins because He has five aces to her royal flush. It seems that there had been a wild card announced, but she had not heard it, being too much in awe of Him. God's winning is a mutual triumph, and she shares God's laughter. God had all the aces, but she has found Him. Thus the seeking of God seems to have a happy ending. She calls Him "dearest dealer" and loves Him for the wild card she did not know about and for His laughter. She seems to be content to lose to God. Indeed, several of the poems in *The Awful Rowing Toward God* seem positive and hopeful in tone, although they are balanced by poems of failure, disappointment, and frustration. Like the movement of oars, the poems go back and forth from possibility to setback, from hope to disappointment.

Analysis. This book did not receive universally positive reviews. Critics recognized the strength of the poems in this collection, but they missed the careful crafting of Sexton's earlier poems. The poems are about God-seeking, but their language is not the language of the church, which may be quirky enough to offend some readers. Moreover, the book appeared shortly after the poet's suicide, which seemed to negate anything positive in its content.

However, there is no question that the poems contained in *The Awful Rowing Toward God* are, in the broadest sense, religious poetry. They are poems of struggle, opposition, and outcry, but they represent a search for God. In them, Sexton mingles her problematic relationship with her dead father with her search for God, and she tries to resolve both.

SOURCES FOR FURTHER STUDY

Middlebrook, Diane Wood. *Anne Sexton: A Biography.* Boston: Houghton Mifflin, 1991.

Morton, Richard Everett. *Anne Sexton's Poetry of Redemption.* Lewiston, N.Y.: Edwin Mellen Press, 1988.

TO BEDLAM AND PART WAY BACK
Genre: Poetry
Subgenre: Confessional poetry
Published: New York, 1960

As with the speaker in *The Awful Rowing Toward God*, the man in Daniel Nevins's 1963 *Crossing* embarks on a symbolic journey, a quest for the spiritual enlightenment that may or may not exist on the other side. In Sexton's poetry, there are no guarantees, and God is often playing with a stacked deck.

Time period: 1950s
Setting: Hospitals; generalized suburban landscapes

Themes and Issues. These poems are a therapeutic response to Sexton's first suicide attempts and her hospitalization for mental illness. The first poem addresses Doctor Martin, who was Sexton's psychiatrist, and describes the inside of the hospital as Sexton experienced it as a patient. Immensely well-crafted, using rhyme and rhythm with originality and skill, these poems nevertheless give a picture of madness that is strange and frightening. The regularity of the rhymes and rhythms makes a stark contrast with the mental instability that remains at their center.

Like the denizens of Telemaco Signorini's 1865 oil painting *Ward for Irritable Patients at San Bonifacio*, the patients at Sexton's institution were herded together and subjected to an often humiliating regimen of group therapy. Many of the poems in her first collection are rooted in helplessness and the self-loathing inspired by life in the mental hospital, where many patients were beyond repair and "where brains rot like black bananas."

tempts within the mental institution to find her way back to sanity.

"Her Kind" remains a favorite among readers, with its strong rhythms and feminist content. The speaker of the poem describes her existence as witchlike, unreal: "I have gone out, a possessed witch/ haunting the black air, braver at night"; the witch woman is at home everywhere and nowhere, fixing supper for worms and elves in the woods, "rearranging the disaligned." She is performing the typical female household chores not in the house, but rather in the woods. In fact, the woman in the poem is really multiple women— witch, housewife, adulteress, and observer—all rolled together. The speaker defines the outcast state of the "different" woman loudly and defiantly and expresses a sisterhood in the refrain "I have been her kind." In later years the poet would form a rock group, Anne Sexton and Her Kind.

"Some Foreign Letters" is based on the correspondence of Sexton's aunt, whom she loved as a mother. This aunt lived with Sexton's family but was taken to a home when she became mentally ill in old age. The poet describes reading letters her aunt wrote "sixty-nine years ago" as a young woman, living an adventurous life in Europe in the 1890s and going on jaunts in Switzerland and Germany with her companion, the count. Unfortunately, "the Count had a wife," and the young woman will grow old and finally come to Massachusetts as "the old maid aunt who lived with us." The speaker feels the collapse of the young girl's exciting life: "You rattled/ down on the train to catch a steamboat for home;/ or other postmarks: Paris, Verona, Rome." Skilled and subtle in its use of rhyme and meter, this poem makes vivid to the reader both who the woman was and who she came to be.

Their themes are mental breakdown, the surroundings of the hospital, the losses that Sexton has experienced, as well as a sense of personal loss and loneliness. Although these are sad poems, they show the poet's recovery from mental illness and her attempts to deal with her losses.

The Poems. The poems in this collection are filled with women, particularly lost, outcast, and lonely women with whom the poet identifies. Three poems that are included in many teaching anthologies are "Her Kind," "Some Foreign Letters," and "Unknown Girl in the Maternity Ward." Each of these focuses on a woman who is unable to find a place in society while retaining her true identity. Other poems convey Sexton's own sense of being outcast as she at-

"Unknown Girl in the Maternity Ward" describes a girl who has had a child outside of marriage and now must give it up to others to raise. Naturally, the pull of motherhood is strong, but society's demands are even stronger, and the woman realizes that she must give the child up. Sexton never had a child out of wedlock, but mental illness separated her from her two daughters. Some of this experience may have gone into the creation of the "unknown girl," who feels the pull of motherhood but will be prevented from acting as her child's mother.

The poem may also have been influenced by Sexton's reading of "Heart's Needle," W. D. Snodgrass's poem about divorce and a custody fight. The girl in Sexton's poem feels the instinctual desire to hold her baby but knows it is for the child's good that she release him: "I touch your cheeks, like flowers. You bruise/ against me . . . We unlearn. I am a shore/ rocking you off. You break from me. I choose/ your only way, my small inheritor. . . . " Again, the craft of the poem is evident. Rhyme and meter serve to carry the flow of the thought.

Analysis. Many first books are quickly surpassed and forgotten, but Sexton's remains a favorite, and some of her most frequently anthologized pieces come from this collection. Others include the poems in which she described the interior life of the mental hospital and her relationship with her psychiatrist. Her book shocked the literary world with its frankness and its breaking of 1950s taboos, despite the formalism of many of the poems. Sexton continued to cause controversy throughout her career, finding new taboos to violate almost as quickly as old ones wore out.

Sexton would later leave rhyme and rhythm for more open forms and entwine life story with myth and folktale, but the relatively simple poems of this first collection continue to strike sparks of recognition in readers who view themselves and their losses in her words.

SOURCES FOR FURTHER STUDY

Hall, Caroline King Barnard. *Anne Sexton.* Boston: Twayne Publishers, 1989.

Middlebrook, Diane Wood. *Anne Sexton: A Biography.* Boston: Houghton Mifflin, 1991.

Other Works

THE DEATH NOTEBOOKS (1974). This poetry collection, published in the year of Sexton's suicide, seems indeed to be notes taken on death. The poems reflect an increasingly angry search for God, and many of them reflect an inability to find either God or some halfway satisfactory substitute. Although the God-seeker finds vacancy everywhere, she continues to search frantically, to look at the world even for the absence of God, to write psalms to God. She refers to herself as Ms. Dog, as Dog is God spelled backward. (Sexton was always fond of such word manipulation.) The psalms in *The Death Notebooks* are odd assemblages of biblical, style phrases, sometimes with similarities to the list poems of Allen Ginsberg. At the end of the collection Sexton does approach the beginnings of an image of God, which she develops more thoroughly, and more poetically, in *The Awful Rowing Toward God.*

LIVE OR DIE (1966). This volume contains mostly directly autobiographical poems in free verse, with a few poems in rhyme. Sexton ordered the poems as they were written in the years from 1962 to 1966, which were for her years of mothering, treatment for mental illness, teaching, and writing. If these poems are less frequently found in anthologies than those of Sexton's earlier collections, it may be because they tend to be long, rambling explorations of inner worlds. They detail with pain and vividness the troubled relationships Sexton had with her mother and with her daughters. The poems suggest that Sexton was never able to find closeness with her mother and seemed to have trouble establishing normal intimacy with her daughters, while acknowledging her need and longing for these special relationships.

The most popular poems from this collection seem to be her mental-illness poems, especially "Wanting to Die," with its explanation of the powerful death wish that obsesses suicidal patients such as Sexton, and "The Addict," a poem about sleeping tablets. "I'm on a diet from death," she says in this poem, which describes the ritual of leaving herself behind that takes place when she swallows eight prescribed tablets each night. The collection does end with an affirmation. The poem "Live" promises the reader that Sexton has been given good things in life and therefore expects to remain here for a while: She has chosen to live, rather than to die. "I say *Live, Live* because of the sun,/ the dream, the excitable gift."

TRANSFORMATIONS (1971). This is an unusual poetry collection, consisting of retellings of fairy tales in such a way as to highlight the roles of the women in them. Sexton does not change what happens to a great degree, but she adds to the stories as she narrates them, giving them strange violent undertones (some are violent already) and suggesting that the traditionally happy endings are unreliable. For example, in Sexton's version of Cinderella, the stepsisters cut off parts of their feet to fit into the glass slipper, then are given away by the leak of blood. This may suggest the lengths to which women went to attract desirable men. At the wedding of Cinderella and the prince, the sisters' eyes are pecked out by "the white dove"—an odd horror—and then "Cinderella and the prince/ lived, they say, happily ever after,/ like two dolls in a museum case/ never bothered by diapers or dust. . . ." The conclusion sounds more coffinlike than blissful.

This pattern persists in the other tales as well. Snow White too becomes the prince's bride, and the wicked queen dances herself to death in iron shoes—but Snow White at the end is described as "rolling her china-blue eyes open and shut/ and sometimes referring to her mirror. . . ." Snow White turns out to be not that different from the wicked queen. This book uses dark humor in its free-verse, untraditional renditions of the fairy tales.

Resources

Much of the Anne Sexton primary materials are in the Anne Sexton Archive at the Harry Ransom Humanities Research Center at the University of Texas in Austin. The archive includes letters, notes, and other materials, but their use is restricted to established scholars.

The Academy of American Poets, Poetry Exhibits, Anne Sexton. The Academy of American Poets has an informative Web site with a selected bibliography of Sexton's work, poems, and links to other Sexton sites. A reading of a poem may be listened to. (http://www.poets.org/LIT/poet/asexton/htm)

Modern American Poetry: Anne Sexton (1928–1974). This Web site, billed as "The Multimedia Companion to *Anthology of Modern American Poetry*," edited by Carey Nelson and published by Oxford University Press (2000), contains a chronology of Sexton's life, critical essays on her work, and a hyperlinked bibliography with graphics of original book jackets and tables of contents. (http://www.english.uiuc.edu/maps/poets/s_z/sexton/sexton.htm)

Anne Sexton and Poetic Confessionalism. This 1999 essay by the poet R. J. McCaffery, written for the online literary journal *Conspire*, discusses Sexton's work and what critics have made of it, in the context of confessionalism. (http://www.conspire.org/rjm0208.html)

Anne Sexton. A fairly extensive Web discussion by Beth Keay, a student, this site includes a poem in draft form and Sexton's discussion of her technique. (http://www.kutztown.edu/~reagan/sexton.html)

JANET MCCANN

Upton Sinclair

BORN: September 20, 1878, Baltimore, Maryland
DIED: November 25, 1968, Bound Brook, New Jersey
IDENTIFICATION: Mid-twentieth-century novelist and journalist known as a "muckraker," whose books exposed the exploitation of the working class.

Upton Sinclair achieved international renown with the publication of his most important work, *The Jungle* (1906), which exposed the unsafe and unsanitary conditions in the Chicago meat-packing industry. His prolific series of novels and nonfiction works challenged corruption and greed and promoted socialism. Sinclair ran for public office several times and was almost elected governor of California. His novel *Dragon's Teeth* (1942), part of his highly popular Lanny Budd series tracing the rise and fall of fascism, won the Pulitzer Prize in 1943.

The Writer's Life

Upton Beall Sinclair, Jr., was born in Baltimore, Maryland, on September 20, 1878. His mother came from a well-to-do Baltimore family, and his father, from a distinguished line of naval officers, turned out to be an alcoholic liquor salesman.

Childhood and College Years. When Sinclair was ten years old, he moved with his family to New York City. He enjoyed an intensive self-education. From the English writer Charles Dickens, he derived his passion for social justice. From another English writer, William Makepeace Thackeray, he got his disdain for hypocrisy and pretense.

Sinclair sped through his secondary education, and in September 1892, he entered the City College of New York before turning fourteen. He supported himself by writing for the monthly magazine *Argosy* and by selling jokes and ideas for cartoons. During this time he also wrote his first, unpublished, novel, *The Prairie Pirates*, which he later confessed bore a striking resemblance to Robert Louis Stevenson's *Treasure Island* (1883). Sinclair graduated from college in 1897 and went to work for *Army and Navy Weekly*, where he produced the remarkable equivalent of a thirty-thousand-word novel weekly.

Early Writing Career. At the turn of the twentieth century, Sinclair moved to Quebec and, working alone for three months, composed and edited a novel, entirely in his head. The resulting book, *Springtime and Harvest* (1901), was an inauspicious beginning to the young writer's career.

The critical indifference to his first novel was an injury to Sinclair's budding ego and a source of shame for his new eighteen-year-old bride, Meta Fuller, whom he had known since they were children. The strikingly beautiful but deeply troubled and unhappy Meta would suffer through eleven years with Sinclair, enduring his meager

By the time he was seventeen, Sinclair, seen here in an undated photograph, was already supporting himself through his writing. He wrote serial adventure tales for several boys' weekly publications, including Cliff Faraday stories, under the name Ensign Clarke Fitch, and Mark Mallory stories, under the name Lieutenant Frederick Garrison.

1378

income and solitary obsession with his work.

The Jungle. Nothing the twenty-seven-year-old Sinclair had done prepared him for the sudden success of *The Jungle*, which catapulted him into the international limelight. Inspired by the 1904 Chicago stockyards strike, his novel would change American society and identify Sinclair as a powerful new voice for social justice.

Originally published serially in the socialist magazine *Appeal to Reason*, *The Jungle* attracted worldwide attention and was recognized as both a literary sensation and a political bombshell. *The Jungle* was a best-seller in the United States and in England for six months and was translated into seventeen languages. President Theodore Roosevelt began receiving one hundred outraged letters a day demanding immediate action. Barely six months after the publication of *The Jungle*, Congress passed the Pure Food and Drug Act and the Beef Inspection Act.

In writing *The Jungle*, Sinclair had wanted to awaken sympathy for the plight of American workers. Instead, most readers were shocked instead by his vivid portrayals of the filth and sickness threatening the U.S. food supply. Sinclair later said: "I aimed at the public's heart and by accident I hit it in the stomach."

Literary Success and Marital Failure. After the publication of *The Jungle*, Sinclair entered a highly productive period. He published a series of novels and nonfiction works, such as *A Captain of Industry* (1906), *The Industrial Republic* (1907), *The Metropolis* (1908), *The Moneychangers* (1908) and *Samuel the Seeker* (1910), exploring a variety of social issues. In 1906 he founded Helicon Hall, a utopian community in New Jersey.

With *The Jungle*, Sinclair's hybrid form of novel and exposé caused a national stir. The book chronicles the struggles of Jurgis Rudkus, a young Lithuanian immigrant who moves to America hoping to strike it rich. Instead, he ends up mired in the filth and "wage-slavery" of the Chicago stockyards.

Despite the steady development of his literary career, Sinclair's personal life was a shambles. His doomed marriage dragged on, sapping any happiness he found in his writing. The only bright spot was the birth of the couple's son, David, in 1903. Against this dysfunctional background, Sinclair wrote *Love's Pilgrimage* (1911), tracing the rise and fall of his marriage.

Sinclair finally divorced Meta in 1911. On April 21, 1913, he married his second wife, Mary Craig Kimbrough, a poet. Their union would last for forty-eight years.

The Dead Hand Series. In 1917 the Sinclairs moved to Pasadena, California. The following year Sinclair began what he called his Dead Hand series, describing the suffocating impact of American institutions on indi-

The publication of *Boston* in the late 1920s, a depiction of the Sacco-Vanzetti case, was yet another sensation set off by Sinclair's roving pen. Here the two Italian immigrants are chained together in a courtroom, awaiting yet another hearing. Still on trial in 1927, Bartolomeo Vanzetti (left) said, "I would not wish to a dog or to a snake, to the most low and misfortunate creature of the earth, I would not wish to any of them what I have had to suffer for things that I am not guilty of."

vidual liberties. Beginning with *The Profits of Religion* (1918), the series included *The Brass Check: A Study in American Journalism* (1919), on the power of the press; *The Goose-Step: A Study of American Education* (1923) and *The Goslings: A Study of the American Schools* (1924), on higher education; *Mammonart* (1925), on Western art and literature, and *Money Writes!* (1927), on the commercialism of contemporary literature.

The ACLU. In 1923 Sinclair was arrested in San Pedro, California, for reading the Bill of Rights at an industrial workers' rally. The international uproar surrounding his arrest led to the founding of the American Civil Liberties Union (ACLU) affiliate in Southern California.

***Oil!* and *Boston*.** In 1927 Sinclair published another best-selling novel, *Oil! A Novel*, to literary and popular acclaim. *Oil!* was banned in the city of Boston for its realistic depictions of the protagonist's sexuality. Slighted by this affront and outraged by the 1927 executions in Boston of Italian immigrant anarchists Nicola Sacco and Bartolomeo Vanzetti, who had been questionably convicted for robbery and murder, Sinclair completed *Boston* (1928) at a feverish pace. Meticulously researched and based largely on the transcripts of the seven-

Sinclair's 1934 campaign for governor of California was his best showing in a political race. He believed that running as a Democrat instead of as a Socialist increased public support for him. In a 1951 letter to Norman Thomas, he wrote, "The American People will take Socialism, but they won't take the label. I certainly proved it in the case of EPIC. Running on the Socialist ticket I got 60,000 votes, and running on the slogan to 'End Poverty in California' I got 879,000."

year criminal proceedings, the novel struck a successful balance between fiction and documentary history.

Taking Stock. At the age of fifty, Sinclair took stock of his life by writing an autobiography, *American Outpost: A Book of Reminiscences* (1932). He waited four years after its completion—until after his mother's death—to publish it. The painfully honest work reveals both his mother's insufferable elitism and the devastating impact of his father's alcoholism.

In 1931 Sinclair published *The Wet Parade*, in which he condemned alcohol and defended Prohibition. It was his only novel to be made into a major motion picture. Metro-Goldwyn-Mayer paid twenty thousand dollars for the rights, and

the film, starring Myrna Loy, Robert Young, Jimmy Durante, and Walter Huston, premiered in March 1932.

Entry into Politics. After losing a 1930 race as the Socialist candidate for governor of California, Sinclair mounted a more serious campaign in 1934. Remarkably, he won the Democratic primary but lost the general election while gaining almost forty percent of the votes. A *Literary Digest* survey placed him fourth on a list of the most outstanding people in the world, behind U.S. president Franklin D. Roosevelt, German dictator Adolf Hitler, and Italian dictator Benito Mussolini.

The Lanny Budd Series. From 1938 to 1948, Sinclair was consumed by an ambitious project. He wrote eleven novels collectively known as the World's End series, or the Lanny Budd series, after its protagonist. The series traced thirty-five years of European history, examining the rise and defeat of fascism. At sixty years old, Sinclair launched a panoramic literary achievement that eventually earned him a Pulitzer Prize and election to the National Institute of Arts and Letters. The Lanny Budd series solidified his international literary reputation and brought him the critical and popular recognition he had long craved.

Final Days. After the death of his second wife, Mary, in 1961, Sinclair remarried the same year. His third wife, Mary Hard, died six years later, in 1967. Sinclair then moved to a nursing home in Bound Brook, New Jersey, to be near his son and daughter-in-law. He died there on November 25, 1968, at the age of ninety. A few years earlier, Sinclair had written his own epitaph: "I don't know whether anyone will care to examine my heart, but if they do they will find two words there—'Social Justice.'"

HIGHLIGHTS IN SINCLAIR'S LIFE

1878 Upton Sinclair is born on September 20 in Baltimore, Maryland.

1888 Moves with family to New York City.

1892 Enters City College of New York.

1893 Supports himself by selling stories, jokes, and cartoon ideas.

1900 Marries childhood friend Meta Fuller.

1903 His only child, David, is born.

1901 Sinclair writes first of five minor books, which earn little money, causing marital tension.

1906 Publishes his most famous novel, *The Jungle*, which hastens the passing of the Pure Food and Drug Act; establishes Helicon Hall, a utopian community in New Jersey that soon burns down.

1911 Divorces his first wife, Meta.

1913 Marries poet Mary Craig Kimbrough.

1917 Moves to Pasadena, California.

1918 Writes first of six books in his Dead Hand series.

1923 Is arrested for reading the Bill of Rights at a labor rally.

1927 Publishes *Oil!*.

1928 Publishes *Boston*.

1930 Makes first of many runs for political office, leading the End Poverty In California (EPIC) movement.

1934 Is defeated as Democratic candidate for governor of California.

1940 Publishes first of eleven novels in his Lanny Budd series.

1943 Receives Pulitzer Prize for *Dragon's Teeth*.

1961 His second wife, Mary Craig, dies; Sinclair marries Mary Hard six months later.

1967 His third wife dies.

1968 Sinclair dies on November 25 in a New Jersey nursing home.

The Jungle by Upton Sinclair

With an Introduction by Morris Dickstein

The Writer's Work

Upton Sinclair was a prolific writer who produced over one hundred novels, nonfiction works, and plays. Best known for his novel *The Jungle*, he was perhaps the most famous of a group of writers known as "muckrakers," a name given them by President Theodore Roosevelt for their works exposing corruption and greed in society. In both his fiction and his journalism, Sinclair advanced his political views and described his dream for a socialist society.

Issues in Sinclair's Fiction.

Throughout Sinclair's novels a single clear pattern emerges. The protagonists are victims of the system; they experience a loss of innocence; they search for a way out; they reject greed and human exploitation; they discover the value of cooperating with society; they sometimes explicitly discover socialism and they enjoy the triumph of idealism.

Perhaps Sinclair was a victim of his own topicality, resulting from his urgent need to expose and to correct problems in contemporary society. Propaganda easily becomes outdated, as the world moves from one war to the next, one political scandal to another. By the 1920's, Sinclair was urgently advocating socialism as the ideal solution to the nation's ills, and by the 1930's he was running, unsuccessfully, for public office as a socialist. The establishment he savaged in his writings found little need to enshrine him in its literary canon.

The Jungle, according to Sinclair, was externally about "a family of stockyard workers, but internally it was the story of my own family." *The Jungle* elevated muckraking from the stuff of special interest magazines into the arena of mainstream book publishing.

Characters in Sinclair's Novels.

Sinclair's best fiction contains vivid characters in realistic settings. Allan Montague, the hero of *Manassas* (1904; revised as *Theirs Be the Guilt*, 1959), is the archetypical Sinclair protagonist: an innocent, good-hearted idealist. He is placed at the center of a surprisingly good historical story revealing the cruelty of slavery.

The novels *The Metropolis* (1908) and *The Moneychangers* (1908) trace the loss of innocence of Allan Montague, son of *Manassas's* hero. A young lawyer from Mississippi, Montague discovers the allure of Fifth Avenue society and the power of Wall Street. He be-

Derricks line the highway at the Signal Hill oil fields in California in this photograph taken around 1930 (left). Considered among Sinclair's most effective writing, *Oil!* casts a critical eye on the booming fortunes of an often-unscrupulous industry. On the right is Sinclair in 1927 with his son, David, looking at a copy of the novel, which was censored in Boston.

comes a part of the ostentatious world of the wealthy, much as Sinclair himself was welcomed by members of New York society enthralled to be in the company of a world-famous radical.

The triumph of idealism over greed and complacency is again on display in *Samuel the Seeker* (1910). When an innocent boy, Samuel Prescott, sees his older brothers destroyed by the manipulation of Wall Street, he decides to track down the wrongdoers. Samuel eventually finds salvation in the socialist underground.

Sinclair the Realist.
Sinclair's highly realistic novels are generally set in contemporary time. They transport readers to the real places where the stories unfold: the Chicago stockyards in *The Jungle*, the California oil fields in *Oil!*, the Italian ghetto in *Boston*, or the homes and offices of wealthy New Yorkers in *The Moneychangers*. Sinclair, who conducted detailed research and copious interviews, prided himself on the accuracy of both his fiction and nonfiction.

Themes in Sinclair's Nonfiction.
When Sinclair wrote not as a novelist but as a reporter, he was liberated from literary pretense or convention. Consequently, he regularly devoted his prodigious research and considerable wit to exposing the threat of "bigness" in American institutions, including government, religion, business, education, and the legal system. His books sounded an urgent alarm that if these institutions continued to grow in size, power, and influence, their exploitation of working people would suffocate individual initiative and personal creativity.

As its name suggests, *The Profits of Religion* gave Sinclair the opportunity to express his unrelenting contempt for organized religion, which he called "a bait, a device to lure the poor into the trap of submission to their exploiters." Sinclair's next book, *The Brass Check*, attacked the American press, charging that "journalism in America is the business and practice of presenting the news of the day in the interest of economic privilege."

Sinclair then turned to the institution of education; *The Goose-Step* examined higher education, and *The Goslings*, secondary schools. Sinclair condemned the role of the establishment, what he called the "interlocking directorate," in controlling education to perpetuate capitalism.

Mixing Fact and Imagination.
In his novels, Sinclair freely mixed real people and fictional characters—a technique known as *roman à clef*—which gave his books an immediacy that proved very popular with readers. In *Manassas*, Sinclair's hero crosses paths with such Civil War–era personalities as the antislavery leader Frederick Douglass, the abolitionist John Brown, the Confederate president Jefferson Davis, and even U.S. president Abraham Lincoln. The fictional characters' interactions with important and familiar political leaders throughout the Lanny

Sinclair's parents, shown here, were extremely poor, but Sinclair as a boy spent periods of time living with his wealthy grandparents. He later argued that witnessing the extremes between these two worlds turned him into a socialist, an advocate for hardworking individuals chained to their cycle of poverty.

Budd series give Sinclair's stories added significance and streamlined his plots.

Propaganda Instead of Plot. Prone to exaggeration and moralizing, Sinclair often overwhelmed his plots with his political and social messages, prompting the criticism that his works were more propaganda than prose. In his nonfiction, Sinclair was often preachy, lecturing rather than informing his readers. This strategy sometimes engendered more sympathy than condemnation for the targets of his attacks.

The breadth of Sinclair's subject matter, which covered virtually every issue of the day, also drew criticism. Sinclair was called a "know-it-all," who nominated himself an instant expert on all his subjects, regardless of his actual expertise. Perhaps inevitably, his passionately held views and the praise he often received for expressing them convinced Sinclair that he knew the true course for the United States. He tended to moralize in his writing, often polarizing issues and ignoring the possibility of validity in his opponents' views.

BIBLIOGRAPHY

Ahouse, John. *Upton Sinclair: A Descriptive, Annotated Bibliography.* Los Angeles: Mercer & Aitchison, 1994.

Blinderman, Abraham, comp. *Critics on Upton Sinclair: Readings in Literary Criticism.* Coral Gables, Fla.: University of Miami Press, 1975.

Bloodworth, William A., Jr. *Upton Sinclair.* Boston: Twayne Publishers, 1977.

Filler, Louis. *The Muckrakers.* Reprint. Palo Alto, Calif.: Stanford University Press, 1994.

Harris, Leon. *Upton Sinclair: American Rebel.* New York: Crowell, 1975.

Herms, Dieter, ed. *Upton Sinclair: Literature and Social Reform.* New York: Peter Lang, 1990.

Jensen, Carl. *Stories That Changed America: Muckrakers of the Twentieth Century.* New York: Seven Stories Press, 2000.

Mitchell, Greg. *The Campaign of the Century: Upton Sinclair's Race for Governor of California and the Birth of Media.* New York: Random House, 1992.

Mookerjee, R. N. *Art for Social Justice: Major Novels of Upton Sinclair.* Metuchen, N.J.: Scarecrow Press, 1988.

Scott, Ivan. *Upton Sinclair: The Forgotten Socialist.* Lewiston, N.Y.: Edwin Mellen Press, 1997.

SOME INSPIRATIONS BEHIND SINCLAIR'S WORK

Upton Sinclair was motivated, both positively and negatively, by his family, his education, his personal experiences, and his lifelong observations of the world around him. Although his alcoholic father and his emotionally distant mother were hardly inspiring, they certainly influenced his poignantly detailed writing describing the suffering his characters endured from loveless marriages and the devastating effects of alcoholism.

Sinclair was genuinely inspired by the strength and nobility of working men and women. The time Sinclair spent living and toiling with packinghouse workers and their families in Chicago gave life and meaning to *The Jungle*. In writing *Oil!* and *Boston*, Sinclair was likewise inspired by the workers and immigrants he grew to know. He sympathized with their plight and felt deeply that his books could help pave the way for a new society.

Another powerful influence on Sinclair was the thousands of letters he received from readers in America and abroad. Sinclair exchanged voluminous correspondence with political leaders, writers, artists, scientists, businessmen, performers, publishers, and common citizens. Through this correspondence, he not only distilled his worldview, but also learned the inner workings of industry, finance, government, education, religion, and other fields. These details found their way into his books, giving them their characteristic sense of realism.

Upton Sinclair and the EPIC Campaign

After three unsuccessful runs for Congress and one unsuccessful race for governor of California, all on the Socialist ticket, in 1934 Upton Sinclair was persuaded to make another run for governor, this time as a Democrat. He won the primary with a majority of the votes in a field of seven candidates and launched what he called "one of the greatest adventures of my life: the EPIC Campaign."

Sinclair on the EPIC (End Poverty in California) campaign trail. In the October 14, 1932, issue of the *Literary Digest*, Sinclair outlined his platform in his race for California governor. He wrote, "The meaning of our movement to End Poverty in California . . . is that our people have reached the saturation point as regards suffering. We are just about to begin the sixth year of the depression. We have one-and-a-quarter million persons dependent upon public charity, and probably as many more who are able to get only one or two days' work a week or who are dependent upon relatives and friends. That is too heavy a burden of suffering for any civilized community to carry."

Poverty in California. Sinclair called it his End Poverty in California, or EPIC, campaign. In a state with a population of seven million, one million were out of work, public relief funds were exhausted, and people were starving.

Sinclair's writing, never far removed from his dreams of socialism, set the stage for his remarkable political challenge. He published two books in 1933, *The Way Out: What Lies Ahead for America?* and *I, Governor of California and How I Ended Poverty: A True Story of the Future*, which outline the principles of the EPIC campaign.

EPIC Principles. Oblivious to any notion of separation of church and state, Sinclair's first principle declared that "God created the natural wealth of the earth for the use of all men, not of the few." He proceeded to announce that when tools of labor become complex, then private ownership becomes enslavement of labor; that "autocracy in industry cannot exist alongside democracy in government"; that the "present depression is one of abundance, not of scarcity"; that the cause of the nation's trouble is that wealth is controlled by a small fraction of society class, while the remainder has only debts; that the "remedy is to give the workers access to the means of production, and to let them produce for themselves, not for the others" and that this change "can be brought about by action of a majority of the people, and that is the American Way."

A Modern Campaign. A measure of how well Sinclair's message began to resonate with average Californians was the fact that he prompted the invention of "negative" political advertising. Concocted by Louis B. Mayer and Irving Thalberg of Metro-Goldwyn-Mayer, fake newsreels were produced and exhibited in theaters, featuring respectable men in the street expressing support for the re-election of Governor Frank Merriam, while vagabonds and men with Russian accents told how eager they would be to go to California if Sinclair were elected to receive relief at taxpayers' expense until they could compete for jobs against hardworking Californians.

For five months, the Sinclair campaign produced an eight-page weekly paper called the *EPIC News*. Sinclair even found the time to write *Depression Island* (1935), a theatrical parable of three castaways on a deserted island filled only with coconut trees. One castaway invents capitalism to control the coconuts and oppresses the other two, until they organize themselves into a union, and then into a government, which passes laws providing for public ownership of the coconut trees. The play was produced on June 27, 1935, at the Shrine Auditorium in Los Angeles and performed elsewhere to enthusiastic EPIC audiences.

Sinclair did not take his opponents' attacks sitting down. Drawing on his skills as a self-publisher, he produced scores of pamphlets and flyers, including "The Lie Factory Starts," in which he charged that "having so bade a case, the opposition has resorted to personalities." He accused those "who hate the Plan because it threatens their privileges" with "deliberate misrepresentations" and announced his intention to "nail a lie as soon as it shows its head." He also al-

Sinclair's message proved hopeful in the lean years of the Great Depression. He proposed, "the State must advance sufficient capital to give the unemployed access to good land and machinery, so that they may work and support themselves and thus take themselves off the backs of the taxpayers." Still, it was not enough to secure him the governor's seat.

leged that the enemies of EPIC would "employ the shrewdest rascals and stop at no crime," including illegally tapping his telephones, using a forged photograph of him trampling on the American flag, and scheming to plant "communistic" literature at one of his headquarters and then staging a raid to "discover" these "seditious documents."

At a time when there were no campaign finance laws restricting political contributions, Sinclair exhibited extraordinary self-restraint, turning down over a quarter-million dollars from insurance companies, corporations, individuals seeking public appointments, and even professional gamblers.

Sinclair vehemently denied the charge that he was a communist or a member of any communist organizations. In particular, he denied that the American Civil Liberties Union was a communist organization, claiming that it "includes the truest and finest Americans in our community, men who are fighting to preserve the American traditions and constitutional rights of freedom of speech, press, and assemblage against the attacks of reactionaries."

On the afternoon before the election, Sinclair spoke at a large rally in Los Angeles. Alluding to his enemies' accusations that vagabonds were coming to the city on freight trains looking for free handouts, Sinclair told his audience that Harry Chandler, owner of the *Los Angeles Times*, had himself come into Los Angeles on a freight train in his youth, and shouted, "Harry, give the other bums a chance!"

A Loss but Not a Defeat. Despite the growing support for his EPIC platform, Sinclair lost the general election with 1,138,620 votes for Merriam, an impressive 879,537 votes for Sinclair, and a pivotal 302,519 votes for the Progressive candidate, Raymond Haight. Ever resourceful, Sinclair turned his political defeat into a literary opportunity. Three days after the election, he began writing his inside account of the campaign, published in 1935 as *I, Candidate for Governor and How I Got Licked*.

SOURCES FOR FURTHER STUDY

Harris, Leon. *Upton Sinclair: American Rebel*. New York: Crowell, 1975.

Mitchell, Greg. *The Campaign of the Century: Upton Sinclair's Race for Governor of California and the Birth of the Media*. New York: Random House, 1992.

Scott, Ivan. *Upton Sinclair: The Forgotten Socialist*. Lewiston, N.Y.: Edwin Mellen Press, 1997.

Reader's Guide to Major Works

BOSTON

Genre: Novel
Subgenre: Political crime story
Published: New York, 1928
Time period: 1920s
Setting: Boston, Massachusetts

Themes and Issues. In *Boston*, Upton Sinclair examines the controversy surrounding the 1927 executions of Italian immigrant anarchists Nicola Sacco and Bartolomeo Vanzetti, who were tried and convicted of robbery and murder. The novel details the notorious trial, based largely on court transcripts, while condemning the pretenses of Boston's ruling class.

The Plot. The novel tells the story of the sensational Sacco-Vanzetti case through the eyes of Cornelia Thornwell, the sixty-year-old widow of Josiah Thornwell, a former Massachusetts governor and a scion of Boston society.

As the novel opens, Josiah has just died, and his three daughters and their husbands have descended on the family home to pay their respects and secure their inheritances. For Cornelia, her husband's death is hardly a tragedy. The daughter of a college professor and granddaughter of an Irish immigrant, Cornelia regrets that being a governor's wife has meant no "charm, or honor, or touch of simplicity! Nothing but heavy pageantry and play-acting from the cradle to the coffin!"

Instead of suffering her daughters' selfishness, on the eve of the reading of Josiah's will Cornelia packs a small bag, takes what cash she has and secretly disappears. She resurfaces in North Plymouth, a factory town south of Boston, where she makes her way to the home of the Brinis, a working-class Italian family. She is welcomed warmly, rents a room, and goes to work making rope at the nearby Plymouth Cordage Company. The work is tedious, and she almost quits but musters the stamina to persist. She meets another boarder, Bartolomeo Vanzetti, a fellow worker who shares his opinions on labor, poverty, ignorance, and capitalism.

Cornelia's granddaughter, Betty, arrives in Plymouth on vacation. Cornelia tells Betty all about her new life and introduces her to the Brinis and to Bart, whom Cornelia calls a "secular saint." While listening to Bart

Adding to Boston's climate of paranoia in 1919, officers prepare to load confiscated piles of literature deemed subversive into a waiting police ambulance. Many now believe the postwar Communist scare and a prevailing suspicion of immigrants all conspired to deny Sacco and Vanzetti a fair trial.

talk about the international workers' struggle and his opposition to fighting wars for capitalists, Cornelia and Betty gradually affirm their pacifism.

Bart introduces Cornelia to his young friend, Nicola Sacco, who works in a shoe factory, and who is equally dedicated to the rights of workers. Bart urges Cornelia that "there are new ideas loose in the world, and it is not practical to keep people from knowing about them."

Betty's mother eventually arrives in Plymouth to convince Cornelia to give up her foolishness and come home. Cornelia agrees to move back to Boston. That fall, Betty enters Radcliffe College and moves in with Cornelia. Together the two attend numerous political meetings. Cornelia goes on the lecture circuit and writes socialist pamphlets. By January of 1920, the government crackdown on labor unions and foreign radicals has escalated, with widespread raids and deportations. Cornelia organizes supporters, raises bail funds, and finds lawyers.

On April 15, 1920, two Italians murder a paymaster and a guard at a shoe factory in South Braintree, Massachusetts, and escape with a sixteen-thousand-dollar payroll. Suspicion turns to Bart and Nick, who are quickly arrested. Bart and Nick claim their innocence but lie to interrogators to protect fellow radicals. Cornelia and Betty raise money to hire an attorney to defend Bart. Betty's boyfriend, journalist Joe Randall, handles publicity, and Cornelia and Betty make speeches to build support.

Sinclair observes that Sacco and Vanzetti "were not going to be tried because they had held up a payroll; they were going to be tried because they were dangerous leaders of social revolt." In the end, both Bart and Nick are found guilty of murder and condemned to death. International outrage grows as the lawyers file no less than nine motions for a new trial, each of which the judge solemnly denies. Appeals to the Massachusetts Supreme Judicial Court and the U.S. Supreme Court are all rejected.

Cornelia and Betty, who is now married to Joe, work frantically but in vain to stop the executions. As protests rage throughout Europe, Cornelia makes her last emotional visits to Bart and Nick, each of whom is electrocuted shortly after midnight on August 22, 1927.

Analysis. *Boston* was a successful and well-reviewed novel, with a powerful literary narrative, well-drawn characters, and sharp observations. Because of the genuine public uproar over the Sacco-Vanzetti case and over the possibility that the men were executed for political reasons, Sinclair's novel avoided the label of propaganda. *Boston* ranks second only to *The Jungle* as Sinclair's finest literary achievement.

SOURCES FOR FURTHER STUDY

Dell, Floyd. *Upton Sinclair: A Study in Social Protest.* Reprint. New York: AMS Press, 1970.

Mookerjee, R. N. *Art for Social Justice: Major Novels of Upton Sinclair.* Metuchen, N.J.: Scarecrow Press, 1988.

Scott, Ivan. *Upton Sinclair: The Forgotten Socialist.* Lewiston, N.Y.: Edwin Mellen Press, 1997.

THE JUNGLE

Genre: Novel
Subgenre: Realistic exposé
Published: New York, 1906
Time period: Early 1900s
Setting: Chicago, Illinois

Themes and Issues. Written to bring public attention to the miserable working conditions in the Chicago stockyards, Sinclair's graphic descriptions of grossly unsanitary meat-processing methods made *The Jungle* an international best-seller. Sinclair devoted months to firsthand research, visiting meat-packing plants and workers' homes to ensure the accuracy of his story. Highly realistic, *The Jungle* weaves contemporary social and economic issues into a dramatic fictional story.

The Plot. As a peasant boy in Lithuania, Jurgis Rudkus falls in love with the lovely, blue-eyed Ona Lukoszaite. Jurgis, hoping to marry Ona as soon as he has enough money, comes to the United States with his father, Antanas, and others. The impoverished immigrants find work in the Chicago stockyards, except for Antanas, who is too old. Jurgis and Ona finally save enough money for their wedding feast and are married in a colorful ceremony.

Antanas works in a wet, cold room, where he develops consumption and dies, but the family has barely enough money to bury him. Jurgis becomes an active member of the union and goes to night school to learn English. Ona

LONG FICTION

1901 Springtime and Harvest
1903 Prince Hagen
1903 The Journal of Arthur Stirling
1904 Manassas (revised as Theirs Be the Guilt, 1959)
1906 The Jungle
1906 A Captain of Industry
1907 The Overman
1908 The Metropolis
1908 The Moneychangers
1910 Samuel the Seeker
1911 Love's Pilgrimage
1913 Sylvia
1914 Sylvia's Marriage
1917 King Coal
1919 Jimmie Higgins
1920 100%
1922 They Call Me Carpenter
1927 Oil! A Novel
1928 Boston
1930 Mountain City
1931 Roman Holiday
1931 The Wet Parade
1936 Co-op
1937 The Flivver King
1937 No Pasaran!
1938 Little Steel
1938 Our Lady
1940 World's End
1941 Between Two Worlds
1942 Dragon's Teeth
1943 Wide Is the Gate
1944 Presidential Agent
1945 Dragon Harvest
1946 A World to Win
1947 Presidential Mission
1948 One Clear Call
1949 O Shepherd, Speak!

1950 Another Pamela: Or, Virtue Still Rewarded
1953 The Return of Lanny Budd
1954 What Didymus Did
1958 It Happened to Didymus
1961 Affectionately Eve

PLAYS

1912 Plays of Protest
1923 Hell: A Verse Drama and Photo-Play
1924 The Millennium
1924 The Pot-Boiler
1924 Singing Jailbirds
1925 Bill Porter
1935 Depression Island
1936 Wally for Queen!
1939 Marie Antoinette
1948 A Giant's Strength

NONFICTION

1904 Our Bourgeois Literature
1907 The Industrial Republic
1911 The Fasting Cure
1918 The Profits of Religion
1919 The Brass Check: A Study in American Journalism
1921 The Book of Life, Mind, and Body
1923 The Goose-Step: A Study of American Education
1924 The Goslings: A Study of the American Schools
1925 Mammonart
1925 Letters to Judd
1927 Money Writes!
1930 Mental Radio
1932 American Outpost: A

Book of Reminiscences
1933 I, Governor of California and How I Ended Poverty
1933 Upton Sinclair Presents William Fox
1933 The Way Out: What Lies Ahead for America?
1934 The EPIC Plan for California
1935 I, Candidate for Governor and How I Got Licked
1936 What God Means to Me
1938 Terror in Russia: Two Views
1939 Expect No Peace!
1952 A Personal Jesus
1956 The Cup of Fury
1960 My Lifetime in Letters
1962 The Autobiography of Upton Sinclair

CHILDREN'S LITERATURE

1936 The Gnomobile: A Gnice Gnew Gnarrative with Gnonsense, but Gnothing Gnaughty

gives birth to a baby boy, named Antanas, after his grandfather. Jurgis sprains his ankle at the plant and, at home for months, soon becomes moody. Desperate, he takes a job in a fertilizer plant and begins to drink. Ona, pregnant again, develops a consumptive cough and goes into fits of hysteria.

To help her family, Ona goes to work at a house of prostitution run by a man named Connor. When Jurgis learns this, he attacks Connor and is sent to jail for thirty days. Alone, Jurgis realizes how unfairly he has been treated by society.

Released from jail, Jurgis searches for his family and finds them living in a run-down rooming house. Ona is in labor with their second child, and Jurgis futilely searches for a midwife, but tragically both Ona and the infant die.

Jurgis tries to find a job but is barred from the stockyards and finally goes to work in a harvesting machine factory. He is soon discharged when his department closes down for a lack of orders. Next he goes to work in a steel mill. To save money, he moves nearer to the mill but can only be home on weekends. One weekend he finds that little Antanas has drowned. After losing his entire family, he escapes from Chicago on a freight train, joining thousands of migratory farmworkers while gaining back his strength.

In the fall, Jurgis returns to Chicago and finds a job digging tunnels. When a shoulder injury costs him his job, he becomes a beggar and is miraculously given a hundred-dollar bill by a wealthy drunk. He goes to a bar to get change, and the bartender tries to cheat him out of his money. In a rage, Jurgis attacks the man and is again sent to jail, where he meets Jack Duane. After their release, Jurgis and Jack undertake several holdups, and Jurgis discovers Chicago's underworld.

When the packinghouse workers demand their rights, and the operators ignore the union, a general strike is called. Jurgis goes to work as a scab. He confronts Connor and attacks him again. This time Jurgis escapes to avoid prison. On the run, he finds Ona's cousin, Marija, working as a prostitute. He is deeply ashamed and angry when he realizes how his whole family has been destroyed.

In a deep state of depression, Jurgis hears a socialist speech in which he finds the answer to the economic oppression he and his family have suffered. At last he learns that workers can find self-respect, and he takes a job in a hotel managed by a socialist. It is the beginning of a new life for Jurgis, the rebirth of hope and cooperation.

Analysis. In *The Jungle*, there is a tension that pervades Sinclair's work, between telling an engaging story and lecturing his readers with political propaganda. This novel is his best-known and most important work because it strikes a successful balance between story and message. Sinclair's gripping and realistic descriptions of the packinghouses rescue the novel from sentimental melodrama. The fact that the novel prompted legislation to improve working conditions and to establish sanitation standards gives it added stature in twentieth-century fiction.

Until the early decades of the twentieth century, few had called into question the often shocking labor standards that prevailed in America—children working instead of being in school, filthy conditions, coercion and thug tactics at the hands of exploitative bosses and owners. With *The Jungle*, what Sinclair thought was a moving tale of the frustrations of young immigrants became in the minds of the public an impassioned plea for reform. Here a child laborer in a dirty dress stands between two giant looms in the 1900s.

SOURCES FOR FURTHER STUDY

Dell, Floyd. *Upton Sinclair: A Study in Social Protest.* Reprint. New York: AMS Press, 1970.

Filler, Louis. *The Muckrakers.* Reprint. Palo Alto, Calif.: Stanford University Press, 1994.

Jensen, Carl. *Stories That Changed America: Muckrakers of the Twentieth Century.* New York: Seven Stories Press, 2000.

OIL!: A NOVEL

Genre: Novel
Subgenre: Realistic exposé
Published: New York, 1927
Time period: 1920s
Setting: Southern California

Themes and Issues. In *Oil!*, Sinclair casts his journalist's eye on his adopted state of California. From the politics and excesses of the oil and motion-picture industries to the flamboyant evangelism of faith healer Aimee Semple McPherson; from the new automobile culture to student life at a fictional Southern California university, Sinclair paints a prophetic portrait of the Golden State.

The Plot. At the center of the novel is young J. Arnold Ross, Jr., known as Bunny, the son of oil magnate J. Arnold Ross, known as Dad. Bunny is an idealist, torn between the privileges of his father's wealth and his own emerging social conscience.

As the story opens, Dad is touring the California oil fields, eager to teach his teenage son about the science and business of oil exploration. When Dad meets with a group of middle-class landowners to acquire their mineral rights, Bunny meets Paul Watkins, a mysterious young man destined to play a pivotal role in Bunny's life.

As oil gushes from Dad's wells, Bunny discovers what it takes to produce such wealth: exploitation. Paul tells Bunny that "the whole world was one elaborate system, opposed to justice and kindness, and set to making cruelty and pain." Dad tells Bunny that business creates jobs, and that, without profits, there would be no jobs.

As World War I rages in Europe, Bunny joins the Army but sees no action. Meanwhile, Paul goes off to war and later complains that "I thought I went into the army to put down the Kaiser, but I was kidnapped by some Wall Street bankers, and put to work as a strike-breaker—a scab."

Fresh from the Army, Bunny enters Southern Pacific University, where he expands his circle of friends linked to the labor movement, including Rachel Menzies, the daughter of Chaim Menzies, a leader among Jewish clothing workers. Bunny meets and falls hopelessly for the vivacious motion-picture actress Viola "Vee" Tracy. The two keep their passionate affair secret, but reality disturbs their idyllic relationship when Vee stars in *The Devil's Deputy*, an epic anti-Russian Hollywood film. At the film's premiere, Rachel condemns Vee for fostering hateful propaganda against the working class. Vee slaps Rachel, forcing Bunny to examine the irreconcilable divisions in his life.

An exposé of corruption in the oil industry prompts a Senate investigation of an oil lease owned by Dad and his business partner, Verne Roscoe, who soon flees to Europe to escape the scandal. After graduating from the university, Bunny begins publishing a newspaper on workers' rights. Paul, now a full-fledged communist, is arrested, and Bunny tries to help his old friend.

Bunny must also help Dad, who is being threatened with a Senate subpoena. Bunny and Dad flee to Vancouver, then to Montreal and London, where they meet up with Verne Roscoe. The expatriates travel to Paris and the Riviera. Along the way, Bunny meets radicals and learns more about the international workers' struggle. He encounters Vee at the opening of her new film, and the two resume their affair.

In Paris, Bunny reconnects with Paul, just returned from Moscow. Paul regales Bunny with stories of the working class and the dream of world government. Bunny confides in Paul his anxieties about Vee. Paul tells Bunny that "you can't have happiness in love unless it's built on harmony of ideas." When Vee issues an ultimatum demanding that Bunny choose between her and his radical friends, Bunny rejects her.

Dad marries a spiritualist from Boston but promises Bunny that his shares in Ross Consolidated, worth one million dollars, are safe. Bunny returns to California by ocean steamer but soon learns that Dad has died of double pneumonia. Because Dad left no will, the second Mrs. Ross claims everything he owned. When Bunny asks Verne for his one million dollars in stock, Verne denies it exists. A messy legal battle ensues.

Bunny survives with only a modest inheritance, which he devotes to a labor college and tent city, a workers' colony to be known as Mt. Hope College. He marries Rachel, the woman with whom he truly enjoys a harmony of ideas. Their happiness is shattered when Paul is beaten during an attack on a union hall. Paul's dying words are "Bread, Peace, Freedom." Inspired by his good friend, Bunny looks forward to a world free of that "evil Power which roams the earth, crippling the bodies of men and women, and luring the nations to destruction by visions of unearned wealth, and the opportunity to enslave and exploit labor."

Analysis. The publication of *Oil!* earned Sinclair both the critical and popular acclaim that had eluded him since the release of *The Jungle*. The novel portrayed vivid characters and genuine relationships with an unmistakable message of promoting socialism.

SOURCES FOR FURTHER STUDY

Harris, Leon. *Upton Sinclair: American Rebel*. New York: Crowell, 1975.

Herms, Dieter, ed. *Upton Sinclair: Literature and Social Reform*. New York: Peter Lang, 1990.

Mookerjee, R. N. *Art for Social Justice: Major Novels of Upton Sinclair*. Metuchen, N.J.: Scarecrow Press, 1988.

Other Works

THE DEAD HAND SERIES (1918–1927). In 1918 Upton Sinclair began what he called his Dead Hand series, six nonfiction works describing the suffocating impact of various American institutions upon individual liberties.

As its name suggests, *The Profits of Religion*, the first of the series, expressed Sinclair's contempt for organized religion, which he called "a bait, a device to lure the poor into the trap of submission to their exploiters."

The next book, *The Brass Check*, focused on the American press. Sinclair charged that "journalism in America is the business and practice of presenting the news of the day in the interest of economic privilege." The book gave examples of news suppression and made a detailed attack on the Associated Press for censoring the news.

Sinclair then turned to the institution of education with *The Goose-Step*, an examination of higher education, and *The Goslings*, a look at secondary schools. These works, like others in the series, are highly autobiographical, drawing on Sinclair's own educational experiences.

In *Mammonart* Sinclair set out to disprove what for him had become a cruel lie—that art was created and justified for art's sake alone. He believed that all art is, and must be, propaganda, dictated by the economic conditions of the time.

Finally, Sinclair focused on his own contemporaries in *Money Writes!*. His hyperbolic style and penchant for preaching obscured the force of his essential message—that capitalism exploited artists as it did all other workers, manipulating their art for the sake of advancing the economic goals of the establishment.

THE LANNY BUDD SERIES (1940–1953). In eleven novels known, for its protagonist, as the Lanny Budd series and also called the World's End series, Sinclair traced thirty-five years of European history and examined the rise and defeat of fascism. In Lanny Budd, his antifascist hero, Sinclair created his most memorable character since Jurgis Rudkus. Lanny Budd, the illegitimate son of a wealthy munitions manufacturer and an international beauty, is a savvy world traveler and art dealer. Lanny moves easily through the halls of power, acting as a secret agent for Franklin D. Roosevelt and meeting with such important international leaders such as France's Henri Philippe Pétain, Germany's Adolf Hitler, the Soviet Union's Joseph Stalin, and China's Mao Zedong.

The first novel, *World's End* (1940), covers the period from 1913 to 1919, including World War I and the Russian Revolution. *Between Two Worlds* (1941) examines the 1920s and the stock market crash of 1929. *Dragon's Teeth*, for which Sinclair won a Pulitzer Prize, traced Hitler's rise to power from 1929 to 1934. *Wide Is the Gate* (1943) covers the mid-1930s, including the appeasement of Germany to forestall its military threat and the Spanish Civil War. *Presidential Agent* (1944) continues the saga of the Spanish Civil War and the Munich Agreement of 1938.

Dragon Harvest (1945) covers Munich, the German victory at Dunkirk, France, and the German Occupation of Paris. *A World to Win* (1946) covers the early 1940s, including the German-puppet government at Vichy, France; the Battle of Britain; and the war in China. *Presidential Mission* (1947) explores the World War II campaigns in Africa and the Pacific and the Allied bombing of Berlin. *One Clear Call* (1948) traces the Allied invasion of Sicily, D-Day, and the reelection of U.S. president Franklin D. Roosevelt.

O Shepherd Speak! (1949) covers the period from 1944 to 1946, including the Yalta Conference ending the war and establishing the United Nations, the death of Roosevelt, and the Nuremberg trials; it also contains an index to the series' first ten volumes. In 1953 Sinclair published *The Return of Lanny Budd*, injecting his hero into the Cold War era.

Resources

The Sinclair Archive of the Lilly Library at Indiana University, Bloomington, Indiana, is the single largest repository of Sinclair's literary work. The archive contains over 1,500 books, pamphlets, and circular letters; about 300,000 pages of personal correspondence; 150,000 pages of manuscripts; 44,000 leaves of manuscripts by Mary Craig Sinclair and masses of clippings, periodicals, secondary books from Sinclair's personal library, tape recordings, and miscellaneous materials. The Upton Sinclair Collection at the Honnol/Mudd Library of the Claremont Colleges contains corrections to the manuscript of Sinclair's autobiography and a collection of his unpublished writings. The John Rylands University Library of Manchester, in Manchester, England, has over 870 monographs in its Upton Sinclair Collection, including first editions of virtually all Sinclair's major works. Other sources of interest for students of Upton Sinclair include the following:

Museum of the City of San Francisco. This museum has an on-line exhibit featuring articles related to Sinclair's political activity in California during the 1930s. Included is an article Sinclair wrote for the *Literary Digest* on the End Poverty in California (EPIC) Movement, articles written by Sinclair's opponents, and correspondence with Jack London, another California author. There are also links to on-line texts of some of Sinclair's titles. (http://www.sfmuseum.org/hist1/sinclair.html)

Study Guides. The Berkeley Digital Library's SunSITE has links to useful study notes for *The Jungle*. (http://sunsite.berkeley.edu/Literature/Sinclair/)

Audio Recordings. A recording of *The Jungle*, read by Robert Morris, is available on audiocassette from Blackstone Audio Books.

STEPHEN R. ROHDE

Isaac Bashevis Singer

BORN: July 14 or November 21, 1904, Leoncin, Poland
DIED: July 24, 1991, Surfside, Florida
IDENTIFICATION: The son of a poor Warsaw rabbi who collaborated
on the translations of his works from Yiddish into English and won the
Nobel Prize in Literature in 1978.

Isaac Bashevis Singer's large output of novels, short stories, memoirs and
other nonfiction, and children's literature made him one of the monumental
figures in twentieth-century literature. Although he was so shocked by
American culture when he settled in Brooklyn, New York, that he could not
write for seven years, he overcame his sense that Yiddish was dead and created a body of original work—much of it first published in the New York
newspaper the *Jewish Daily Forward*—that preserves the culture he knew as a
child and at the same time speaks to eternal questions about God and hu-
mankind.

The Writer's Life

Isaac Bashevis Singer was born in Leoncin, Poland, on either July 14 or November 21, 1904; he himself said that he had two birthdays. His father, Pinchas Mendel Singer, was a Hasidic rabbi whose judgments in his rabbinical court, or *beth din*, at 10 Krochmalna Street in Warsaw are recounted in Singer's absorbing memoir *Mayn Tatn's Bes-din Shtub* (1956; *In My Father's Court*, 1966). Pinchas Mendel was a pious, impractical, and unworldly man of faith, the descendant, his family claimed, of a long line of distinguished rabbis. Singer's mother, Bathsheba Zylberman Singer, was the daughter of the rabbi of Bilgoray, Poland—he was a *Mitnagged*, or enlightened Jew, from a tradition stressing reason, the law, and learning. The contrast between the opposing sensibilities of Singer's parents—the rational mother and the spiritual father—emerges in Singer, the talented son whose own thinking can be described as a struggle between the two visions. Pinchas Mendel triumphs eventually, but the repeated references to the seventeenth-century rationalist philosopher Baruch Spinoza reveal the persistent temptations of cool reason.

Childhood. Singer's parents lived first in Bilgoray, Poland, where his sister, Hende Esther, was born in 1891 and his brother Israel Joshua in 1893. The family soon moved to Singer's future birthplace, Leoncin, and to Warsaw in 1908. Singer would later draw upon the awful poverty of his childhood on Krochmalna Street in Warsaw. His experience of intense exposure to life glows in such works as *In My Father's Court* and *A Day of Pleasure: Stories of a Boy Growing up in Warsaw* (1969), with photographs by Roman Vishniac of daily life among Warsaw's Jews.

Scene showing poverty in Warsaw, Poland, 1904–1919.

Early Influences. In 1917 Singer moved with his mother and younger brother, Moishe, to Austrian-occupied Bilgoray, where he met his mother's family. Old Jewish customs seemed preserved in Bilgoray, which was also permeated with talk of Zionism, socialism, and economic revolution. This atmosphere astonished and stimulated Singer, who later attributed the atmosphere of his first novel, *Der Sotn in Gorey* (1935; *Satan in Goray*, 1955) to his experiences there. The characters Rechele and Rabbi Benish in that novel owe much to his Aunt Rochele and his Uncle Joseph. It was in Bilgoray that Singer first studied Hebrew and published stories in a Hebrew newspaper, much to the disapproval of his stern Hasidic relatives.

For his book *A Day of Pleasure: Stories of a Boy Growing Up in Warsaw*, Singer won a National Book Award in the children's book category in 1969. Here he poses at Philharmonic Hall in New York City with winners in other categories: (left to right) Dr. Erik H. Erikson, Lillian Hellman, Joyce Carol Oates, and Singer. This photograph was taken on March 4, 1970, when the awards presentation was held.

At the same time, Singer was saturating himself in the works of Jewish writers such as Sholom Aleichem and Isaac Leib Peretz, as well as reading Yiddish translations of such Russian masters as Anton Chekhov and Leo Tolstoy. After four years in Bilgoray, he returned to Warsaw to study at Tachkemoni Rabbinical Seminary, an experience that after a year left him virtually starving. At this time he read a book that was to be one of the most influential on his own career, Knut Hamsun's *Sult* (1890; *Hunger*, 1899).

Apprenticeship. In 1923 Singer was living with Moishe and his parents in the village of Dzikow, when his brother Israel Joshua offered him a job as proofreader on the Warsaw journal *Literarishe Bletter* (*Literary Pages*), for which Israel Joshua wrote. Singer was contemptuous of the contents of *Literary Pages*, and he despised his work, but he found solace at the Writers' Club and the library.

He supplemented his income by translating books by Hamsun, Stefan Zweig, Erich Maria Remarque, and Thomas Mann into Yiddish. Although he considered the merits of the Hebrew language, Singer settled on Yiddish—a High German dialect enriched by words from Hebrew and the Slavic languages, written in Hebrew characters, and spoken as a vernacular by Eastern European Jews and others who immigrated abroad. His first story, "In Old Age," in Yiddish, was published in *Literary Pages* in 1927. More stories appeared under several pseudonyms, one of them "Isaac Bashevis," from Bas-Sheva, the Yiddish form of his mother's name, Bathsheba.

Searching for Love. Singer's memoirs record a life history of multiple and concurrent romantic entanglements that inspired the stories of such fictional characters as Asa Heshel Bannet of *Di Familye Mushkat* (1950; *The Family Moskat*, 1950), Aaron Greidinger of *Neshome Ekspeditsyes* (1974; *Shosha*, 1978), and Hertz Grein of *Shadows on the Hudson* (1998). Singer admitted to having been influenced by the nineteenth-century Austrian misogynist writer Otto Weininger and said that no marriage should last more than fifteen years. In his early years in Warsaw, Singer spent time at the Writer's Club in the shadow of his brother Israel Joshua and enjoyed an in-

Singer, who wrote in Yiddish, was awarded the Nobel Prize in Literature in 1978 for the body of his work. In this photograph, taken on December 9, 1978, he appears with other 1978 Nobel winners at the Royal Academy of Science reception in Stockholm, Sweden. Singer is second from the left, with his face turned away from the camera.

(1945–1948) of *The Family Moskat* in the *Forward*. Three years later Saul Bellow translated Singer's story "Gimpel the Fool" into English for the *Partisan Review*, and Singer's career writing in Yiddish was fully underway.

The Nobel Celebrity. Two decades of steady publishing, including two National Book Awards, led to Singer's being awarded the Nobel Prize in Literature in 1978. The honor was significant not only for the acclaim it bestowed upon Singer personally, but also for what many viewed as its validation of Yiddish as a literary language. Much was made of the view that Singer's work preserved memories of a way of life extinguished by the Holocaust—an interpretation that added resonance to the award. The editor of the *Forward*, Shimen Weber, seized fast to the tails of Singer's Nobel tuxedo, stressing that "The *mazltov* we gave Bashevis is also a *mazltov* for all of us—writers and readers of Yiddish." Although Singer affected diffidence about the prize, he apparently greatly enjoyed being a "Big Shot," as he mockingly described himself, even though the subsequent celebrity drove him to obtain an unlisted phone number.

tense affair with a much older woman whom he calls Gina Halbstark in his memoirs.

In *A Young Man in Search of Love* (1978), Singer recounts his concurrent affairs with the servant girl in his apartment and with Stefa Janovsky, who wanted him to marry her and go to Palestine—a chapter in his life fictionalized in *The Certificate* (1992). His romance with the communist Runya led to the birth of his only child, Israel Zamir, whom he abandoned when he left for New York. Singer always loathed communism and its Warsaw intrigues, and no permanent relationship with the leftist Runya was ever possible. His 1940 marriage to Alma Haimann endured, but it is clear that Singer's promiscuity, for which he made no excuses, continued.

Adrift in New York. Singer's first decade in the United States, to which he had followed his brother Israel Joshua in 1935, was generally an ordeal during which he struggled to gain confidence writing in Yiddish. He scraped by with contributions to the Yiddish newspaper the *Jewish Daily Forward*, finally publishing four significant stories in 1943. He achieved a major breakthrough with the serial publication

Coda. Singer continued to write after the momentous Nobel Prize year, but his significant work was behind him, partly because of his age, but partly because he was spending unaccustomed amounts of time consulting on the conversion of several of his works into other media. By the late 1980s Singer had been diagnosed with Alzheimer's disease, and his wife, Alma, struggled to care for him in their Miami home. He died in the Douglas Gardens Rest Home in Surfside, Florida, on July 24, 1991, and was buried in New Jersey.

The Writer's Work

Isaac Bashevis Singer said, more than once, that readers should not look for messages in his work. In fact, the reasons he outlined for writing for children illuminate his intentions in everything he wrote and make a useful introduction to any discussion of his fiction. Singer pointed out that children read books, not reviews. Moreover, they do not read to find their identities, to free themselves of guilt, to quench their thirst for rebellion, or to avoid feelings of alienation. They do not expect authors to redeem humanity. They have no use for psychol-

FILMS BASED ON SINGER STORIES

1979 *The Magician of Lublin*

1983 *Yentl*

1984 *The Cafeteria*

1989 *Enemies: A Love Story*

1997 *Aaron's Magic Village*

One of Singer's unique individuals who tried to control her fate is the character Yentl in his 1974 play *Yentl, the Yeshiva Boy.* This photograph shows Barbra Streisand in the film adaptation as Yentl, a young woman at the turn of the century who has to disguise herself as a man in order to pursue an education and study the Torah.

ogy or sociology; they still believe in intangibles such as God, angels, devils, witches, and goblins. They love interesting stories, not commentary or footnotes, and they appreciate clarity, logic, and proper punctuation. If a story bores them, they will yawn openly.

Allegory and Realism. Despite Singer's declared preference for readers who still believe in angels, witches, and "other such obsolete stuff," many of his works, especially short stories such as "The Gentleman from Cracow," are clearly sophisticated allegories. Tales of imps and devils, in fact, form one pole of Singer's literary imagination, balanced against such strictly realistic narratives as *Shadows on the Hudson*. In a prefatory note to *Sonim, de Geshichte fun a Liebe* (1966; *Enemies: A Love Story*, 1972) Singer explains that "the characters are not only Nazi victims but victims of their own personalities and fates." This remark, and others similar in spirit, reveals a writer who aims to tell, without comment or judgment, stories that follow unique individuals through human entanglements over which they have little control.

Singer differs from naturalistic novelists such as Theodore Dreiser in that he leaves readers to decide for themselves what cosmic significance should be read into the lives of his floundering characters. Despite Singer's refusal to pass judgment on his characters, his characterizations are so believable and his convincing dramatic situations are often so painful and harrowing that he cannot suppress his conclusions about the point of existence. Something of Singer's own feelings emerges in his observation that God is apparently powerful but not merciful.

Singer's Sex-Obsessed Characters.
The erotic content of Singer's work goes mainly unremarked in the mainstream of modern fiction, but it has not always been so with Singer's Yiddish readers,

many of whom were troubled by the relentless, sex-driven behavior of his heroes. Singer's men pursue multiple relationships with a nearly pathological disregard for commonsense restraint, and the women present themselves with a sexual hunger that often humiliates them.

Asa Heshel Bannet strides on stage in *The Family Moskat* prepared to conquer the world, but he squanders his opportunities and abilities in a series of fruitless relationships with women. Like the compulsive womanizer Abram Shapiro, one of old Moskat's sons-in-law, Asa Heshel finds his

Safed, Israel, where the Kabbala, Judaism's foremost mystical text, was written in the second century by Rabbi Shimon Bar-Yochai, is a center for Jewish learning. In this 1988 photograph, which evokes the characters in some of Singer's works, Richard T. Nowitz has captured two pairs of Hasidim, unaware of each other, involved in discussions in an alley in the mystical city.

HIGHLIGHTS IN SINGER'S LIFE

1904   Isaac Bashevis Singer is born in Leoncin, Poland.

1908   Moves with family to Warsaw.

1917   Moves with mother and younger brother to her hometown of Bilgoray.

1918   Teaches Hebrew in Bilgoray and begins writing in that language.

1921   Spends a year at Tachkemoni Rabbinical Seminary in Warsaw.

1923   Works in Warsaw as a proofreader for the Yiddish literary journal *Literary Pages*; translates modern fiction writers into Yiddish.

1925–1927 Publishes several Yiddish stories in Warsaw magazines.

1929   Fathers a son, Israel Zamir, by his communist mistress, Runya.

1934   Publishes first novel, *Satan in Goray*, in installments in *Globus*.

1935   Moves to Brooklyn, New York, and abandons writing in Yiddish for seven years.

1940   Marries Alma Haimann.

1943   Resumes writing in Yiddish.

1944   Older brother, the novelist Israel Joshua Singer, dies.

1945–1948 Singer publishes *The Family Moskat* in installments in the *Jewish Daily Forward*.

1950   Publishes *The Family Moskat* in book form in both Yiddish and English.

1953   Saul Bellow translates the short story "Gimpel the Fool" into English for *Partisan Review*.

1955   Singer meets his son, Israel Zamir, for the first time in twenty years.

1957   Publishes first collection of short stories in translation, *Gimpel the Fool and Other Stories*.

1964   Is elected to National Institute of Arts and Letters.

1967   His novel *Der Hoyf* (1953–1955; *The Manor*, 1967) is nominated for the National Book Award.

1970   Wins National Book Award for children's books for *A Day of Pleasure: Stories of a Boy Growing Up in Warsaw*.

1974   Wins National Book Award for *A Crown of Feathers and Other Stories* (1973).

1978   Receives Nobel Prize in Literature.

1984   Is inducted into Jewish-American Hall of Fame.

1986   Receives Handel Medallion, New York City's highest award.

1990   Is elected to the American Academy of Arts and Letters, the only member ever inducted who did not write in English.

1991   Dies on July 24 in Surfside, Florida.

Many of the forty-nine short pieces in Singer's *In My Father's Court* describe incidents from the rabbinical court conducted by his father in their home in Warsaw. Max Weber's *The Talmudists,* 1934 (The Jewish Museum, New York, New York), showing rabbis studying and interpreting the Talmud, on which all codes of Jewish law are based, evokes the scenes that were part of the young Singer's life and had a great influence on his writing.

world of Eastern European Jews, especially that of the pious Hasidim. The essentials of the youthful Singer's everyday world—the men's gaberdines, or long cloaks, the boys' sidelocks, and the devotion to the Torah and other holy works—all bespeak a way of life unfamiliar even to most contemporary Jews. Hasidic laws about such matters as diet and the preparation of food— laws that have little apparent reference to empirical reality in the contemporary world—give structure, meaning, and purpose to a world of chaos and constant menace from the non-Jewish world. The clash of this world with twentieth-century secularism must have been difficult for many of those who experienced it.

BIBLIOGRAPHY

Alexander, Edward. *Isaac Bashevis Singer.* Boston: Twayne Publishers, 1980.

Allison, Alida. *Isaac Bashevis Singer: Children's Stories and Childhood Memories.* New York: Twayne Publishers, 1996.

Goran, Lester. *The Bright Streets of Surfside: The Memoir of a Friendship with Isaac Bashevis Singer.* Kent, Ohio: Kent State University Press, 1994.

Hadda, Janet. *Isaac Bashevis Singer: A Life.* New York: Oxford University Press, 1997.

Kresh, Paul. *Isaac Bashevis Singer: The Magician of West Eighty-sixth Street.* New York: Dial Press, 1979.

Malin, Irving, ed. *Critical Views of Isaac Bashevis Singer.* New York: New York University Press, 1969.

_____. *Isaac Bashevis Singer.* New York: Frederick Ungar, 1972.

Miller, David Neal, ed. *Recovering the Canon: Essays on Isaac Bashevis Singer.* New York: Brill Academic Publishers, 1986.

Singer, Isaac Bashevis, and Richard Burgin. *Conversations with Isaac Bashevis Singer.* Garden City, N.Y.: Doubleday, 1985.

Zamir, Israel. *Journey to My Father, Isaac Bashevis Singer.* Translated by Barbara Harshav. New York: Arcade Publishing, 1994.

only solace in flesh, as if no other escape exists in a world of constant madness and suffering. No innocent maidens are debauched by Singer's men; instead, men and women meet, lust, agonize, and separate in paroxysms of mutual need and repulsion. The material circumstances of their lives are incidental to their torments: The prosperous Hertz Grein of *Shadows on the Hudson* is no less helpless than Asa Heshel.

Cultural Context. Singer's Polish works, such as *In My Father's Court* and *The Family Moskat,* graphically depict the claustrophobic

Isaac Bashevis Singer on Stage and Screen

Several of Isaac Bashevis Singer's works have been turned into plays or films, including the film versions of *The Magician of Lublin* (1979) and the more acclaimed *Enemies: A Love Story* (1989), but none of them proved so problematic for Singer as Barbra Streisand's film version of the short story "Yentl the Yeshiva Boy." Singer's story features a girl, Yentl, who wants so badly to study the Torah like the men that she disguises herself as a boy and takes the name Anshel to gain entrance to the yeshiva. The story becomes rather preposterous, given the difficulties she must overcome.

Yentl becomes close friends with a young man, Avigdor, whose marriage to the lovely Hadass is thwarted by her parents. Yentl herself marries Hadass as a kind of surrogate for Avigdor. This absurd masquerade goes on for several months until Yentl reveals the truth to the shocked Avigdor. No one else knows the facts, and the townspeople are stunned when divorce papers are delivered to Hadass. Avigdor then divorces his shrewish wife and finally marries Hadass himself. The couple name their son Anshel.

"Yentl the Yeshiva Boy" on Stage. The Broadway production of *Yentl* opened at the Eugene O'Neill Theater on October 23, 1975, in a version written by Leah Napolin and Singer himself

Singer published *The Magician of Lublin* in 1960, and it was made into a film in 1979, starring Alan Arkin, Louise Fletcher, Valerie Perrine, Shelley Winters, and Lou Jacobi. This photograph shows Alan Arkin as the Magician having just completed a routine in his magic act.

and directed by Robert Kalfin. Yentl was played to great acclaim by Tova Feldshuh. The cross-dressing theme was resisted by many people, not only because of its improbability but also for religious reasons. Singer resisted commenting on his intent regarding gender issues or Yentl's significance for feminism, and the story really needs no elaborate search for meaning. The wedding night is muffled in one obscure sentence, and there is preaching about women's rights: Yentl is simply a young woman who wants to study the Torah. In the original story, Yentl just disappears and life goes on, but the stage version has a different ending, at which Singer himself had sneered, citing the vulgarity of the American Yiddish theater. Despite the changed ending, much care went into guaranteeing verisimilitude in the setting, even to the extent of hiring a rabbi to instruct the cast in nuances of ritual and understanding.

Streisand's Yentl. Singer teamed up with Barbra Streisand for the film version of "Yentl the Yeshiva Boy," but Streisand did not like the script he wrote and discarded it to write her own. This annoyed Singer, who had already complained that she had bought the rights for "a bargain," but Singer was powerless since he had sold the rights. Moreover, Streisand had her own ideas and was unlikely to be swayed, not even by a Nobel Prize winner.

Singer was so unhappy about the film, which premiered on November 18, 1983, that he interviewed himself for *The New York Times*. His main complaints concerned Yentl's trip to America at the end of the movie, and Yentl's singing. What would Yentl do in America, he asked? Live in the Bronx "with an ice box and a dumbwaiter"? Yentl was motivated by a desire to learn, Singer insisted, and Streisand had completely distorted his intentions in the story. Could one imagine, he asked, Madame Bovary on the Riviera or Anna Karenina married to an American capitalist?

Singer "never imagined Yentl singing songs." Although Singer did not mention the Orthodox objections to hearing a woman sing, other Jewish scholars have noted that the identification of a woman's voice as a source of sexual stimulation had led many Orthodox authorities to ban women from singing, especially in the company of men. For Singer, Streisand's deliberate flouting of such a strong prohibition was morally reprehensible.

Streisand kept aloof from the controversy, but her supporters' letters to the *Times* blasted Singer for his self-interview and criticism of *Yentl*. Singer must have been extremely annoyed by his encounter with a full-size media star, but whatever he thought of Streisand's one-woman show—as writer, producer, director, and star—she created a larger audience than he could have expected from his own efforts. Moreover, in filming the story of Yentl and the yeshiva, she dramatized for millions of viewers the world that Singer had preserved in fiction.

"Enemies: A Love Story." After the controversy surrounding Streisand's successful *Yentl*, the film version of *Enemies: A Love Story*, written by Roger Simon and directed by Paul Mazursky, was a major success, undisturbed by controversy. Mazursky was conscientious about details, even having the actors eat in Jewish delicatessens, and his efforts paid off. Singer biographer Janet Hadda recounts Mazursky's story of his first meeting with Singer: "And he said, 'I deedn't like what Barbra Streisand did with *Yentl*.' So I said, 'Mr. Singer, I promise you—no songs.' 'You're a good boy,'" Singer replied.

SOURCES FOR FURTHER STUDY

Berman, Saul J. "Kol `Isha." In *Rabbi Joseph Lookstein Memorial Volume*, edited by Leo Landsman. New York: KTAV, 1980.

Hadda, Janet. *Isaac Bashevis Singer: A Life*. New York: Oxford University Press, 1997.

Singer, Isaac Bashevis. "I. B. Singer Talks to I. B. Singer About the Movie *Yentl*." *The New York Times*, January 29, 1984, p. 2A.

Reader's Guide to Major Works

THE CERTIFICATE

Genre: Novel
Subgenre: Apprenticeship novel
Published: New York, 1992
Time period: 1922
Setting: Warsaw, Poland

Themes and Issues. *The Certificate* features questions about the Jewish nationalist movement of Zionism that advocated the Jews' relocation to Palestine, but it also dramatizes grimly the fate of Jewish communists who left Poland to work for the Soviet cause. Isaac Bashevis Singer castigates these naïve Jews for abandoning one rigid system, Judaism, for the even more rigid system of communism.

Singer's lifelong fascination with the philosopher Baruch Spinoza continues as the novel's protagonist, David, ponders Spinoza's *Ethics* and puzzles over fate and free will in the awful injustices humans suffer. David's sex life is ambitious and muddled, with him musing "that by means of sex one made contact with the *Ding an Sich*, the raw material of phenomena with the seed of truth that is concealed by the intellect's illusions." These are all familiar subjects in Singer's fiction.

The Plot. David Bendiger, an eighteen-year-old would-be writer, arrives in Warsaw, Poland, in 1922 seeking his fortune, and his earnest strivings often have comic consequences. He immediately stumbles into a common scheme of the time— marrying a woman simply to put her on a certificate, or visa, to relocate in Palestine. His fictive spouse is Minna Ahronson, who is eager to join her real fiancé, Zbigniew Shapira, and begin a new life. While waiting to leave with Minna, David lives in a bedbug-infested room belonging to two communists, Bella and her niece, Edusha. Both women have sanctimonious Jewish communist lovers, and Bella and her lover soon end up in prison.

David's older brother, Aharon, returns from Russia with grim news of events there, and he introduces David to the Writers' Club. While David is consorting with an old acquaintance,

This oil-on-cardboard painting *Pogrome,* ca. 1915 (Judaica Collection Max Berger, Vienna, Austria), by an unnamed artist, shows Jewish refugees fleeing after a pogrom in Russia. Although the painting and this particular pogrom predate the overthrow of Czarist Russia, the painting reflects Singer's views and fears expressed in *The Certificate* for the fate of Polish Jews who went to Russia in the belief the Communist revolution could benefit them.

Sonya, as well as with Edusha, his marriage partner, Minna, is jilted by her Zbigniew, a terrible blow that falls immediately after the confiscation of all the Ahronsons' furnishings by the tax authorities. When Minna hears from Zbigniew again, she rushes to him in Danzig. Upon her return she gushes to David that Zbigniew and his new wife want her to travel with them in a *ménage* and even to bring David with them.

SOME INSPIRATIONS BEHIND SINGER'S WORK

The most powerful influences on Isaac Bashevis Singer's work were clearly his mother, the rationalist from a Bilgoray family of devotion to the law and learning, and his father, the pious but unworldly Hasidic rabbi whose steady procession of visitors with problems introduced the young Singer to human behavior and to the culture of the Jews under oppression in Warsaw. Singer's brother, Israel Joshua, succeeded as a writer long before the younger Isaac, and although his style and subjects did not influence Singer he was a constant presence in Singer's consciousness.

Of all the writers Singer read, Baruch Spinoza, a seventeenth-century Sephardic Jew from Amsterdam, United Provinces (now The Netherlands), made the deepest impression, as is obvious from Singer's almost obsessive allusions to Spinoza in many works. Spinoza's *Ethica* (1677; *Ethics*, 1870) presents a God who is not transcendent and anthropomorphic but immanent; that is, one in whom God and nature are one and the same, as Spinoza asserts in remarks such as "Whatever is, is God" and "If anything is, God is."

Spinoza's rejection of free will was answered by Singer with frequent declarations of Singer's belief in human existential freedom. However, the written evidence suggests that Singer must have struggled to achieve this belief. His preoccupation with Spinoza suggests a lifelong dialogue in his own mind over the merits of rationalism.

Singer once spoke of having read the eccentric German cultural thinker Otto Weininger when he was young and of how Weininger's misogynism probably had a good deal to do with his callousness toward the many women who were attracted to him. Other writers who left strong impressions on Singer included Knut Hamsun, the Russian novelist Fyodor Dostoyevski, and the German philosopher Immanuel Kant.

Isador Kaufmann's oil-on-canvas painting *Friday Evening,* ca. 1920 (The Jewish Museum, New York, New York), embodies the major influences on Singer's life and work: his mother and Orthodox Jewish culture and customs.

Meanwhile, the arrival of David's father in Warsaw revives in David old questions of religious faith. When the novel ends he is through with Warsaw and waiting at the train station for a ticket back to Byaledrevne, the town he had recently left.

Analysis. *The Certificate* treats familiar Singer themes: the young man bedeviled by intellectual doubt, entangled with several women simultaneously, and trapped in a quickly changing world that is about to disappear in the horror of the Holocaust. Palestine looms in the background as a refuge that is never fully endorsed by Singer, and the communists receive Singer's usual contempt, especially those Jewish intellectuals who "out-poped the Pope" in their allegiance to Moscow: "The Yiddish Communists had transformed atheism into a form of Hasidism—the same inward look, the same telling of moral tales, the same repetition of Torah and the idolatry of their rebbes."

Sexual desire is presented as irrational and obsessive, a force that seemingly justifies the prohibitions taught by the rabbis. David recognizes the spiritual sickness that has sapped his strength but can find no foundation upon which to sustain belief: "But how could one maintain the purity of the family without believing that the Torah was given to the Jews on Mt. Sinai?" David's apparent opting out as he departs on the train at the novel's end symbolizes the hopelessness of the Eastern European Jews' situation as Hitler and Stalin grew stronger and stronger.

SOURCES FOR FURTHER STUDY

Alexander, Edward. *Isaac Bashevis Singer*. Boston: Twayne Publishers, 1980.

Hadda, Janet. *Isaac Bashevis Singer: A Life*. New York: Oxford University Press, 1997.

Singer, Isaac Bashevis. *A Young Man in Search of Love*. New York: Farrar, Straus and Giroux, 1978.

THE FAMILY MOSKAT
Genre: Novel
Subgenre: Family chronicle
Published: New York, 1950

Time period: 1915–1939
Setting: Warsaw, Poland

Themes and Issues. *The Family Moskat* is a six-hundred-page chronicle of the fortunes of the Warsaw patriarch Meshulam Moskat, his seven children by the first two of his three wives, and all the in-laws, lovers, and others in the Moskat family orbit. Asa Heshel Bannet, a young scholar from the village of Tereshpol Minor, comes to Warsaw with a copy of Spinoza's *Ethics* in his pocket and immediately finds himself swirling in the wake of the Moskat family's turbulent course.

The combined stories of Asa Heshel and the Moskats span the early years of the twentieth century right up until World War II, depicting the lives of Eastern European Jews before the Holocaust changed their world brutally and irrevocably. The characterizations are vivid, and the human dramas are enacted with great narrative skill against a rich cultural background.

The Plot. Old Moskat dies soon after his third marriage, leaving his descendants without his strong, unifying presence. By his first wife, Moskat had four children: Joel, Pearl, Hama, and Nathan; by his second wife, three: Pinnie, Nyunie, and Leah. Of these the most prominent are Hama, whose husband, Abram Shapiro, is a congenial, womanizing, good-for-nothing man; Nyunie, married first to Dacha, by whom he has a daughter, Hadassah, and then to Bronya Gritzenhendler; and Leah, married first to Moshe Gabriel Margolis and then to her father's conniving assistant, Koppel Berman.

Asa Heshel Bannet has distinguished ancestors, especially in his grandfathers, Reb Dan Katzenellenbogen and Reb Jerachmiel Bannet, a man of "fervent and inordinate piety." Koppel Berman and his first wife, Bashele, have four children: Manyek, Shosha, Yppe, and Teibele. The Berman brood play lesser roles, but Koppel's machinations contribute much to the Moskat family's disintegration. Koppel emerges as the sly underling, of undistinguished background, whose energy and watchfulness enable his cynical rise in the world.

Marc Chagall's *The Rabbi* (Galleria d'Arte, Moderna, Venice, Italy) embodies the essence of Reb Meshulam Moskat, the patriarch of Singer's six-hundred page chronicle *The Family Moskat.*

his wife and lives with Leah for several years in America, where he turns to bootlegging.

Asa Heshel soon marries Adele Landau, daughter of Rosa Frumetl Landau, Meshulam Moskat's third wife, but the marriage fails and Asa Heshel makes his way back to Hadassah, now married to Fishel Kutner. Their affair becomes a family scandal as first Adele bears Asa Heshel's son, David, and then Hadassah his daughter, Dacha.

The protracted relationship of Asa and Hadassah—they finally marry—eventually exhausts them both, and Asa takes up with a sophisticated "parlor radical," Barbara Fishelson. The novel ends a quarter-century after old Moskat's death with Hitler's bombing of Warsaw. Asa Heshel is still with Barbara, Adele has joined her son in Palestine, Hadassah is dead from a bomb, and Koppel Berman and Abram Shapiro have both succumbed to heart attacks.

When Asa Heshel meets Abram Shapiro quite by accident, he is immediately taken up by the irresponsible Abram and introduced into the Moskat family circle. By the time Reb Meshulam Moskat dies, a third of the way through the novel, Asa Heshel has run off to Switzerland with Nyunie's daughter, Hadassah, who is arrested at the border and returned to her parents to marry the Reb's choice for her, a decent but boring young man named Fishel Kutner. In the confusion of the Reb's final sickness, Koppel Berman plunders the patriarch's safe and leaves the children squabbling over scraps of an inheritance. Berman later divorces

Analysis. Asa Heshel's personal story dominates the narrative. Adele asks herself as she leaves him for good on her way to Palestine how could such a talented young man from the provinces come to Warsaw and fail to achieve the distinction expected of him. Her answer is eloquent: "He was one of those who must serve God or die. He had forsaken God, and because of this he was dead—a living body with a dead soul." In Adele's answer lies the explanation for Asa Heshel's constant search for sexual gratification: As he contemplates leaving Barbara, Asa Heshel realizes that "his existence was too gray; he simply had to find something to hang on to."

Asa Heshel's story and the other complicated personal relationships work themselves out against a somber background. In the collapse of the Moskats and the failure of Asa Heshel Bannet can be seen the erosion of the forefathers' piety under pressure from Enlightenment reason and secularism. The Hasidic faithful are diminished, leaving a small gathering presided over by Fishel Kutner. The Nazi menace, always in the back-

LONG FICTION

1935   Der Sotn in Gorey (Satan in Goray, 1955)
1950   Di Familye Mushkat (The Family Moskat, 1950)
1953–1955 Der Hoyf (The Manor, 1967, and The Estate, 1969)
1958–1959 Der Kuntsnmakher fun Lublin (The Magician of Lublin, 1960)
1961   Der Knekht (The Slave, 1962)
1966   Sonim, de Geshichte fun a Liebe (Enemies: A Love Story, 1972)
1974   Neshome Ekspeditsyes (Shosha, 1978)
1974   Der Bal-Tshuve (The Penitent, 1983)
1988   Der Kenig vun di Felder (The King of the Fields, 1988)
1991   Scum
1992   The Certificate
1994   Meshugah
1998   Shadows on the Hudson

SHORT FICTION

1957   Gimpel the Fool and Other Stories
1961   The Spinoza of Market Street
1964   Short Friday and Other Stories
1968   The Séance and Other Stories
1970   A Friend of Kafka and Other Stories
1973   A Crown of Feathers and Other Stories
1975   Passions and Other Stories
1979   Old Love
1982   The Collected Stories
1985   The Image and Other Stories
1988   The Death of Methuselah and Other Stories

PLAYS

1973   The Mirror
1974   Yentl, the Yeshiva Boy (with Leah Napolin)
1974   Shlemiel the First
1978   Teibele and Her Demon

NONFICTION

1956   Mayn Tatn's Bes-din Shtub (In My Father's Court, 1966)
1976   A Little Boy in Search of God: Mysticism in a Personal Light
1978   A Young Man in Search of Love
1980   Lost in America
1980   Reaches of Heaven: A Story of the Baal Shem Tov

CHILDREN'S LITERATURE

1966   Zlateh the Goat and Other Stories
1967   The Fearsome Inn
1967   Mazel and Shlimazel: Or, The Milk of a Lioness
1968   When Shlemiel Went to Warsaw and Other Stories
1969   A Day of Pleasure: Stories of a Boy Growing up in Warsaw
1970   Elijah the Slave
1970   Joseph and Koza: Or, The Sacrifice to the Vistula
1971   Alone in the Wild Forest
1971   The Topsy-Turvy Emperor of China
1972   The Wicked City
1973   The Fools of Chelm and Their History
1974   Why Noah Chose the Dove
1975   A Tale of Three Wishes
1976   Naftali the Storyteller and His Horse, Sus, and Other Stories
1980   The Power of Light: Eight Stories
1982   The Golem
1984   Stories for Children

ground, has exploded into the terror that was to become the Holocaust, and as more and more of Warsaw falls in ruins the last words are spoken by the communist Hertz Yanovar: "Death is the Messiah. That's the real truth."

SOURCES FOR FURTHER STUDY

Buchen, Irving. *Isaac Bashevis Singer and the Eternal Past.* New York: New York University Press, 1968.

Davidowicz, Lucy S. *The Golden Tradition: Jewish Life and Thought in Eastern Europe.* Boston: Beacon Press, 1967.

Saposnik, Irving. "Translating *The Family Moskat.*" *Yiddish* 1 (Fall 1973): 26–37.

SHOSHA

Genre: Novel
Subgenre: Love story
Published: New York, 1978
Time period: 1914–1951
Setting: Warsaw, Poland; Israel

Themes and Issues. To describe *Shosha*, originally published in Yiddish as *Neshome Ekspeditsyes*, simply as a love story is inadequate. It is that, but it is also a commentary on history, on God's purpose, and on how people should live their lives. The love story is easiest to account for: Aaron Greidinger, the narrator, explains that he loves and marries Shosha, the simple friend of his childhood, because she is the only woman whom he can trust. Shosha's frailness and her illiteracy are of no consequence in light of the unquestionable goodness of her heart, and Aaron tells one of his sophisticated mistresses that what he

sees in Shosha is himself—himself as he was years before when he and she were innocent children growing up together in the poverty of Warsaw's Krochmalna Street.

The goodness of Shosha's love contrasts with the brutality of life that Aaron sees everywhere in the hell of the slaughterhouses that "made mockery of all blather about humanism." A restaurant scene of tables loaded with roasted animals surrounded by gorging patrons suggests a painting by twentieth-century German Dadaist George Grosz: "Bellies protruded, necks were thick, and bald pates gleamed like mirrors. The women chattered vivaciously, laughed, and dug their red fingernails into the portions of fowl that couldn't be got at by a fork." Finally, the love story is enriched by the numerous passages on metaphysics that appear throughout the narrative, especially the meditations by the idle scholar and true mensch, Morris Feitelzohn.

The Plot. Aaron Greidinger is a writer who after two decades returns to visit Shosha, his

The character Feitelzohn in Singer's *Shosha* sees Coney Island as a metaphor for a world of hedonism, a world where everything is a game. John Wenger's *Coney Island,* 1931 (Brooklyn Museum of Art, Brooklyn, New York), although painted during the Great Depression, reflects that view.

childhood friend of the pre-World War I period, and marries her, much to the delight of her family and the astonishment of his literary friends. This straightforward story is interwoven with Aaron's simultaneous relations with four other women. Dora Stolnitz is a Communist Party functionary for whose ideology Aaron expresses great contempt. Celia Chentshiner is the wife of Haiml Chentshiner, a homosexual who nevertheless maintains a loving relationship with Celia while allowing her complete freedom. Betty Slonim is a fading actress from New York who travels with her rich lover, the much older Sam Dreiman, and for whom Aaron attempts to write a chaotic play about a woman possessed by two dybbuks, or wandering souls. Tekla is the gentile maid in Aaron's apartment. All love Aaron, all forgive him his infidelities, and all get along with each other and accept Shosha as his wife.

In the epilogue set in Israel in 1951, Aaron encounters his old friend Haiml. Their conversation reveals that Shosha died the second day after leaving Warsaw with Aaron and that only Haiml is left from the group of Aaron's Warsaw friends. The tone of this epilogue is elegiac and moving. Aaron Greidinger appears again in the novel *Meshugah* (1994).

Analysis. The novel's story should not overshadow its philosophical speculation. The shrewd character Feitelzohn, a postmodernist ahead of his time, admires the eighteenth-century Scottish philosopher David Hume and sees in Coney Island a metaphor for a world of hedonism in which all activity is a game. Feitelzohn insists eloquently that "The day will come when all truth will be recognized as arbitrary definitions, all values as rules of a game." He sees theoretical mathematics much the way he sees Einstein's theories of relativity—"Nothing but wordplay." Feitelzohn's elaboration of his religious theory is answered by Haiml with warmth: "If God needs a Hitler and a Stalin and icy winds and mad dogs, let Him have them. I need you, Morris, and you, Tsutsik [Aaron], and if there is no merciful truth, I take the lie that gives me warmth and moments of joy." These unconnected asides make *Shosha* a love story that engages life on many fronts.

SOURCES FOR FURTHER STUDY

Alexander, Edward. *Isaac Bashevis Singer*. Boston: Twayne Publishers, 1980.

Alter, Robert. "Shosha." *The New Republic*, September 16, 1978, 20–22.

Miller, David Neal, ed. *Recovering the Canon: Essays on Isaac Bashevis Singer*. New York: Brill Academic Publishers, 1986.

Other Works

THE COLLECTED STORIES (1982). This volume includes forty-seven stories chosen by Isaac Bashevis Singer from the more than one hundred that he wrote. He repeats in a brief "Author's Note" an aesthetic similar to the one he stated in his reasons for writing for children, with a special contempt for "so-called 'experimental' writing." In his emphasis on the need for brevity and a "definite plan" for the short story, Singer sounds like Edgar Allan Poe. Singer's insistence that "genuine literature informs while it entertains" is a credo as old as Horace's *Ars Poetica* (ca. 17 b.c.e.; *The Art of Poetry*, 1567).

Although Singer never alludes to the nineteenth-century New England novelist Nathaniel Hawthorne, there are many parallels between their works. Both authors create allegories of good and evil often set on some ambiguous boundary between the real and the fantastic, and both reveal a conviction that in the race for salvation a warm heart conquers an all-devouring intelligence. The cosmic pessimism that colors most of Singer's fiction receives overt statement in the summary remark that "at its best, art can be nothing more than a means of forgetting the human disaster for a while." He adds that he is "still working hard to make this 'while' worthwhile."

None of Singer's stories better illustrate the parallels between himself and Hawthorne than "The Gentleman from Cracow." This fable tells of a visit to the destitute town of Frampol by Ketev Miri, Chief of the Devils. The citizens of Frampol struggle along with no blessings other than those of their handsome young people. With starvation threatening the villagers, a carriage pulls up one day bearing an elegant young man dressed in the finest clothes. He explains that he is a doctor and a widower, so tremendously rich that he will finance a luxurious life for the townspeople. Moreover, he will arrange an unprecedented ball at which he will choose his wife from all the eligible young women. Despite the protestations of Rabbi Ozer, preparations go on, with each young woman being guaranteed a bridegroom on the great occasion, and "although the young men still sat in the study house poring over the Talmud, its wisdom no longer spoke to them."

Hodel, a drunken outcast living on the edge of Frampol, receives the same finery for the occasion as the other women, and when the gentleman from Cracow chooses her as his bride, she reveals herself as an unrepentant blasphemer. An old man in the crowd is gagged when he shrieks warnings to the impious revelers. As the gentleman from Cracow takes Hodle, the archetypal Lilith, by the hand to dance, rain, hail, and "mighty thunderclaps" emerge from the offended sky. Lightning destroys the synagogue, the study house, and the ritual bath simultaneously as the gathering degenerates into an orgy and all the wicked creatures from Satan's legions descend on the scene.

Rabbi Ozer gradually revives the corrupted inhabitants of the now swampy Frampol, and good people from a nearby town donate food and necessities. A new Frampol develops over the years, with a new rabbi, and the villagers respond to any exorbitant price from a tradesman with the imperative, "Go to the gentleman from Cracow and he will give you buckets of gold."

A representative New York story, "The Yearning Heifer" is a witty example of Singer's view of sexual psychology. The story follows a young man from Brooklyn to a week's stay at a farm that he has found advertised in the Yiddish newspaper for which he writes. The farm turns out to be run-down, with inhospitable hostesses in a mother and daughter who sulk for having been moved there from the city. A black heifer bawls constantly in the barnyard. The women say the heifer needs a bull, and the nature-loving husband and father retorts that her misery derives from having just been taken away from the other animals on a neighboring farm. The visitor hears in the heifer's lament "the despair of everything that lives."

The tense domestic situation lightens up considerably when the women learn that the visitor writes a column that they regularly read, and everybody's joy leads to their all walking to the neighbor's farm to return the yearning heifer, who slips placidly in among the herd. That evening, with everyone contented, the husband and wife retire to bed "with the gay anticipation of a young couple," and the columnist and the farmer's daughter go for a walk as the night rains meteors over their heads. The sky is luminous. "It yearned with a cosmic yearning for something which would take myriads of light-years to achieve."

As the couple embrace, the columnist narrates, "Her wide mouth bit into mine like the muzzle of a beast," and "I heard a blaring sound, mysterious and otherworldly, as though a heavenly heifer in a faraway constellation had awakened and begun a wailing not to be stilled until all life in the universe shall be redeemed." This brilliant story dramatizes the sexual ethic that reigns everywhere in Singer's work: that humans clutch at each other's bodies from a desperate need to calm the anguish that afflicts them from birth.

IN MY FATHER'S COURT (1966). Originally published in Yiddish in the *Jewish Daily Forward* as "Mayn Tatn's Bes-din Shtub" under the pseudonym Isaac Warshawsky, many of the forty-nine short pieces in this memoir describe incidents from the *Beth Din*, or rabbinical court, conducted by Singer's father in their home. Singer explains the Beth Din as "a kind of blend of a court of law, synagogue, house of study, and, if you will, psychoanalyst's office where people of troubled spirit could come in to unburden themselves." Each rabbi, Singer says, "colored [the Beth Din] with his character and personality." For the young Singer, lurking around the fringes of these often vivid dramas in his own home at 10 Krochmalna Street, the Beth Din was a remarkable education in human behavior and a wealth of source material for a writer in the making.

"The Secret" describes one of the more vex-

ing cases for Singer's father, which dealt with a woman who had borne an illegitimate child forty years earlier and had abandoned it on the steps of a church, leading to its having been raised, presumably, as a gentile. Years later, married and settled with her family, she is overcome with guilt at the thought of what a sinner the child may have grown up to be. The kind rabbi agonizes over the woman's misery and assigns her a penance of fast days, psalm recitations, and contributions to charities.

The young Singer hears something from the woman that stays in his mind: the belief that illegitimate children become firemen and are forbidden to marry so that they can always be on call for a fire. Soon after, a house burns across the street and Singer is sure he can iden-

When Singer was growing up on Krochmalna Street in Warsaw, Poland, his father, Pinchas Mendel Singer, a poor Hasidic rabbi, conducted a rabbinical court in his home. Singer wrote about the incidents that occurred in this court on a daily basis in his memoir *In My Father's Court*. Edouard Moyse's *Rabbinic Dispute* (Musée de Judaisme, Paris, France) captures a dramatic moment in such a rabbinical court.

tify the woman's son among the firemen. Then he begins to obsess over the possibility that he too is a foundling, startling his mother by asking if he is really her son. The story illustrates the effect on a young imagination of the confessions common in a rabbinical court.

In "The Purim Gift" the revelry of the feast of Purim, held about a month before Passover, is contrasted with the normal asceticism of the pious Jewish puritans among whom Singer grew up. The feast of Purim caused his father some stressful moments. Neighbors sent presents of food and drink all day long, but the pastries could not be eaten because they could have been cooked with chicken fat, which could not be eaten with milk foods.

The rabbi did serve the wine to the Hasidim, but the label on a bottle of English ale was too worldly, depicting a red-faced man with a feather in his hat whose "intoxicated eyes were full of a pagan joy." His father's rueful comment was, "How much thought and energy they expend on these worldly vanities." Singer observes that the great world outside their home was *tref*, or unclean, and adds this crisp judgment: "Many years were to pass before I began to understand how much sense there was in this attitude."

Resources

Sources of interest to students of Isaac Bashevis Singer include the following:

Audio Recordings. There are numerous recordings of Singer reading his work. Two titles on the Caedmon label are *Isaac Bashevis Singer Reading His Stories*, which includes such stories as "Gimpel the Fool" and "The Man Who Came Back," and *Isaac Bashevis Reads in Yiddish*, which features such stories as "Klein und Grois" ("Big and Little"), "Shiddah un Kuzibah" ("Shiddah and Kuziba"), and "Der Zurickgeshriggener" ("The Man Who Came Back").

Isaac Bashevis Singer Read by Eli Wallach is a recording from the Spoken Arts label, featuring the stories "The Séance" and "The Lecture." Another recording featuring the voice of Eli Wallach is *Eli Wallach Reads Isaac Bashevis Singer*. This title features Singer's children's stories; from *Zlateh the Goat and Other Stories* (1966) are "Fool's Paradise," "The Snow in Chelm," "The First Shlemiel," and "Zlateh the Goat." From *When Shlemiel Went to Warsaw and Other Stories* (1968) are "Shrewd Todie and Lyzer the Mizer," "Rabbi Leib and the Witch Cunnegunde,"

and "When Shlemiel Went to Warsaw." This title was released by Newbery Award Records.

Khazaria Info Center Bookstore. This Web site features a large collection of books about Eastern European Jews with capsule summaries and ordering information. (http://www.khazaria.com/eejbooks.html)

Carpati: Fifty Miles, Fifty Years. This film, written and directed by Yale Strom and narrated by Leonard Nimoy, focuses on a contemporary Jewish ice cream vendor living in a small town in the Carpathian Mountains of the Ukraine, a region where a quarter of a million Jews once lived. The video is available for purchase through its Web site. (http://www.remember.org/carpati/)

Hasidic Stories Home Page. This Web site is devoted to the appreciation and sharing of Hasidic stories. Every month, a new story by a contemporary storyteller, rabbi, or other authority on Hasidic stories is featured. (http://www.storypower.com/hasidic/)

FRANK DAY

Gertrude Stein

BORN: February 3, 1874, Allegheny, Pennsylvania
DIED: July 27, 1946, Paris, France
IDENTIFICATION: Early twentieth-century writer of radical novels, plays, poems, and essays, best known for *The Autobiography of Alice B. Toklas* (1933).

Gertrude Stein, known as the "mother of modernism," was at the center of the Paris art world between 1903 and 1940. She introduced the world to revolutionary new styles in painting and literature and befriended and entertained many of the key painters, writers, and personalities of the era. Her writing, which defies genre categorization, was for the most part ignored and even mocked in her lifetime, but she nevertheless became a celebrity and literary icon late in her life. She enjoyed her greatest success and fame in her last years with the publication of her memoirs.

Gertrude Stein was born on February 3, 1874, in Allegheny, Pennsylvania. She was the last of seven children, two of whom died before she was born. Her father, Daniel Stein, quarreled with his brothers, his partners in a textile business in Pittsburgh, and took the family to Europe in 1875. Over the next five years, the family moved twice, leaving Stein with memories of life in Vienna and Paris, the city to which she eventually returned and in which she made her permanent home. Her father, a broker and capitalist, was successful enough to support his family in comfortable style, but he was dissatisfied with life in Europe and

Stein with her brothers Leo and Michael (with cigarette) in 1904. Of her childhood, Stein would write, "There you are privileged, nobody can do anything but take care of you, that is the way I was and that is the way I still am, and any one who is like that necessarily liked it. I did and I do."

brought his family back to America, finally settling in Oakland, California, in 1880. There Stein spent most of her childhood and teenage years in a close friendship with her next older brother, Leo.

Childhood. When Stein was eleven, her mother, Amelia, was diagnosed with cancer. Amelia remained an invalid for the next three years, and the Stein children had to learn to care for one another; Amelia died when Stein was only fourteen. Three years later, Stein's father also died, leaving the five children orphans. The oldest of the children, Michael, took over the management of the family's interests and was successful enough to provide his siblings with a modest income. Stein, then only seventeen, continued her close companionship with Leo.

College Years. In 1893, soon after Leo left Oakland to attend Harvard University, Stein followed him there. She enrolled at the Harvard annex for women, which was later renamed Radcliffe College, but she did not receive a degree. Leo graduated with a degree in philosophy but was unable to settle into the field. He became restless, leaving the United States to travel around the world.

In 1897 Stein continued her education, studying medicine at Johns Hopkins University and eventually obtaining her bachelor's degree. Leo returned from his trip, and they lived together while Stein pursued graduate studies in psychology. Stein's first romance was with another student, May Bookstaver. It was an unhappy relationship, as Bookstaver was involved with another student. Stein lost interest in her studies and failed several of her classes in her last year of school, 1901, partially because of the stress and soul-searching caused by her romantic affair. Although she studied medicine for years, she had no interest in practicing medicine professionally.

The Salon. Stein began writing fiction at this time, as she began to write about her affair with Bookstaver in notebooks. Her medical career plans abandoned, Stein fled to Europe in 1903, where she joined Leo, and together they toured Italy and England. They settled in Paris, sharing an apartment on their allowances from the family business. They began buying paintings by adventuresome young artists, who in many cases could not find other buyers for their art. Stein and her brother filled their walls with original works by the then-unknown artists Paul Cézanne, Henri Matisse, and Pablo Picasso. As friends' interest in their collection grew, they began to host regular Saturday night salons, meetings of interesting people who gathered to look at the paintings and discuss new trends in art.

Alice B. Toklas, who was to become Stein's lifelong companion, left San Francisco after an earthquake devastated the city in 1906 and came to Paris to visit a friend. In 1907 she met Stein. The two were soon inseparable and moved in together in 1910. Leo was comfortable with this domestic arrangement at first, but tension grew between him and Stein over his lack of understanding of her writing. He moved out in 1913.

After Leo's departure, Stein continued the Saturday salons.

Whereas Leo had never supported Stein's writing, calling it "bosh," Toklas learned to type in order to transcribe the notebooks that Stein filled by hand. Stein spent time every day writing, enjoying the support of her new companion. She was not as successful in attaining the respect of the publishing world, however, and never saw much of her work in print. Toklas wrote to publishing houses on Stein's behalf, but Stein's early novels were rejected on both

Gertrude entered Radcliffe College in 1893. There she studied with the eminent philosopher William James, who openly acknowledged her as his "ideal student." During the final exam in James's course, she wrote at the top of her paper, "Dear Professor James, I am sorry but really I do not feel a bit like an examination paper in philosophy today." The next day she received a note from James saying, "I understand perfectly how you feel. I often feel like that myself." He gave her the highest mark in his course.

sides of the Atlantic. Stein and Toklas decided to turn to private publishing and began paying for publication themselves. The public's lack of understanding of her work was disappointing to Stein, but she displayed an indomitable sense of her own importance and worth, declaring herself a genius and "the only important writer of the twentieth century."

World War I. Around 1908, Stein turned to writing "word portraits" of her friends. These were more accessible than her novels and found publication in journals and private pub-

lications. In 1914 her book *Tender Buttons: Objects, Food, Rooms*, a revolutionary work of cubist literature, was published. It was the same year that World War I broke out, trapping Stein and Toklas in England. Unable to return to Paris, Stein and Toklas moved instead to Mallorca, Spain, where they spent the war years isolated from the artistic world. As the tide of war turned in 1916, they returned to Paris.

Stein asked a friend to teach her to drive and then obtained a truck, the first of many Fords that she and Toklas were to own. The pair

Stein and Toklas pose with their dog, Basket, in 1944 in front of the château in which they lived during the four years of Nazi occupation during World War II. Toklas holds the manuscript of Stein's latest book.

spent the last years of the war driving around France delivering supplies for the American Fund for French Wounded. They spent much of their own money to help make the soldiers comfortable, providing them with cigarettes, blankets, and clothing. Stein was rewarded with the Medaille de la Reconnaissance Française for this service after the war ended in 1918.

In the 1920s Stein and Toklas returned to the salon life of Paris with some of their old friends and many new ones. Stein was friendly with many of the most innovative writers, painters, and poets of the growing modernist movement in art and literature.

Fame.
Stein enjoyed a reputation as the writer to know in Paris, but her work continued to be unmarketable. Toklas, distraught over Stein's lack of financial success, demanded that Stein write a commercial book, a book of memoirs, and Stein did. *The Autobiography of Alice B. Toklas* was a huge hit in America, and Stein finally returned to her homeland for a triumphant lecture tour, drawing large audiences and receiving celebrity treatment from the dazzled press.

Stein and Toklas returned to Europe flush with money and the pride of vindication. When World War II began, their lives became difficult, as they chose to stay in occupied France, living out the entire war in their summer house in Belignin. Stein and Toklas emerged unscathed in 1945, and Stein ended her career writing successful books and articles about the war. However, her health was fading, and in 1946, at the age of seventy-two, she died during surgery for cancer.

In 1916 Stein and Toklas decided to help out with the war effort by joining the American Fund for French Wounded. Stein is seen here aiding soldiers. A car, nicknamed Auntie in honor of Stein's aunt, was shipped from America and outfitted like a truck so they could deliver supplies to hospitals around Paris.

HIGHLIGHTS IN STEIN'S LIFE

1874	Gertrude Stein is born on February 3, in Allegheny, Pennsylvania.
1875	Moves with family to Vienna, Austria.
1880	Returns with family to United States, settling in Oakland, California.
1888	Amelia Stein, Stein's mother, dies of cancer after three years of illness.
1891	Daniel Stein, Stein's father, dies.
1893	Stein enrolls at Harvard's women's annex.
1898	Receives bachelor's degree in medicine from Johns Hopkins University.
1900	Begins affair with May Bookstaver; summers in France and Italy with brother Leo.
1901	Fails graduate course work at Johns Hopkins University; gives up medicine.
1903	Affair with Bookstaver ends; Stein moves to Paris to be with her brother Leo.
1905	Stein and her brother begin buying paintings.
1907	Stein and Alice B. Toklas meet in Paris.
1910	Toklas moves into Stein's Paris apartment.
1912	Stein publishes "word portraits" of Picasso and Matisse in *Camera Work*.
1913	Leo moves out of the Paris apartment.
1914	*Tender Buttons* is published in London; Stein lives with Toklas in Mallorca, Spain.
1916	Begins traveling with Toklas through France, delivering supplies to the needy.
1925	Publishes *The Making of Americans*.
1929	Rents summer house in Belignin, France, with Toklas.
1933	Publishes *The Autobiography of Alice B. Toklas*, which becomes a best-seller.
1934	Returns to United States for lecture tour.
1940–1944	Remains in occupied France during World War II.
1945	Publishes *Wars I Have Seen*; entertains American soldiers in Paris.
1946	Publishes *Brewsie and Willie*; is diagnosed with cancer; dies on July 27 during surgery for cancer in Paris, France.

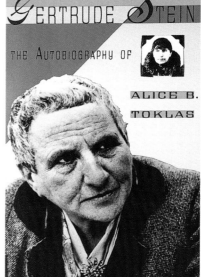

The Writer's Work

Gertrude Stein produced a vast amount of writing. Yale University, to which she bequeathed her manuscripts, lists more than six hundred titled works. Many of her works were never published in her lifetime, but she intended that all of her writing eventually be made available to the public. The stylistic variety of Stein's writing is remarkable as well. She produced plays, poems, novels, essays, lectures, memoirs, and children's books.

Abstraction. Some of Stein's work is unusual in that it does not attempt to describe a scene, tell a story, or relate an opinion or point of view. These works are more like attempts to render abstract paintings in written form. Stein's friends Picasso and Matisse made paintings that did not fool viewers into thinking they were seeing objects through windows, for example, but instead looking at paint applied to flat surfaces. In a similar fashion, Stein made literature consisting of words on a page, referring only to itself, not to some other place or reality.

Many of Stein's works are puzzling. Passages and even entire works are unclassifiable, freely mixing styles of prose, poetry, and drama. It is impossible to categorize Stein's work because of the variety of styles that she utilized in her career.

Writing Techniques. One of Stein's most famous prose devices is repetition; in her sentences words are repeated, sometimes in subtly different order, sometimes for entire, long paragraphs. This device appears frequently in her word portraits and in *The Making of Americans*. Her most famous quote, "A rose is a rose is a rose is a rose," is an example of this device, for which she was parodied and ridiculed.

One reason that much of Stein's writing is perceived as difficult is that her mature writing does not use many of the standard marks of

Stein's Paris address for more than forty years, 27 Rue de Fleurus, became the nucleus of the city's art scene. Literary and artistic luminaries, such as the French painter Henri Matisse, seen here, were frequent guests at her salons.

punctuation other than the period. She felt that punctuation only led the reader along by manipulating an emotional reaction, something she was not interested in doing. In her conversational works, she does not make use of quotation marks or identify the different speakers, effectively blurring distinctions between dialogue and narrative.

Continuous Present. Much of Stein's writing relates to the twentieth-century style of writing known as "stream of consciousness," which attempts to describe the interior monologue of the mind. Some critics accused Stein of playing nonsense games in her writing, but she was a scientifically trained psychologist. She may not have graduated or practiced professionally, but she did apply her interest in and understanding of the workings of the human mind in her daily life.

In Stein's mature period much of her output can be seen as an attempt to describe the sensation of consciousness, an attempt to delve into personality, examining it at great length. Her first published writing was a thesis on psychology. Her next writings that found their way into

LONG FICTION

1909 Three Lives
1925 The Making of Americans
1930 Lucy Church Amiably
1931 Before the Flowers of Friendship Faded, Friendship Faded
1932 A Long Gay Book
1939 The World Is Round
1940 Paris, France
1941 Ida: A Novel
1946 Brewsie and Willie
1948 Blood on the Dining-Room Floor
1950 Things as They Are (published later as Quod Erat Demonstrandum)
1952 Mrs. Reynolds and Five Earlier Novelettes, 1931–1942
1958 A Novel of Thank You
1971 Fernhurst, Q.E.D., and Other Early Writings

NONFICTION

1926 Composition as Explanation
1931 How to Write
1933 The Autobiography of Alice B. Toklas
1933 Matisse, Picasso, and Gertrude Stein, with Two Shorter Stories
1934 Portraits and Prayers
1935 Lectures in America
1935 Narration: Four Lectures
1936 The Geographical History of America
1937 Everybody's Autobiography
1938 Picasso
1940 What Are Masterpieces
1945 Wars I Have Seen
1973 Reflections on the Atomic Bomb
1974 How Writing Is Written

PLAYS

1922 Geography and Plays
1932 Operas and Plays
1934 Four Saints in Three Acts
1946 In Savoy: Or, Yes Is for a Very Young Man (A Play of the Resistance in France)
1947 The Mother of Us All
1949 Last Operas and Plays
1951 In a Garden: An Opera in One Act
1968 Lucretia Borgia

1970 Selected Operas and Plays

POETRY

1914 Tender Buttons: Objects, Food, Rooms
1948 Two (Hitherto Unpublished) Poems
1953 Bee Time Vine and Other Pieces, 1913–1927
1956 Stanzas in Meditation and Other Poems, 1929–1933

CHILDREN'S LITERATURE

1939 The World Is Round

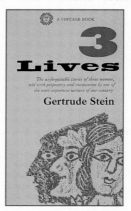

1424

Rene Magritte's 1939 *La Bonne Parole* (The Good Word) reflects the role of symbolism and imagery that Stein's work calls into question. Some critics view her famous quote "A rose is a rose is a rose is a rose" as an attempt to strip words of the associations and connotations they acquire, and thus effectively blur their meanings.

Stein's early novels, *Q.E.D.* (written in 1903 and published in 1971; also published as *Things as They Are* in 1950), *Fernhurst* (written in 1904–1905 and published in 1971), and *Three Lives* (1909) represent attempts to write in an acceptable, traditional style. Some of Stein's idiosyncrasies are present, but, for the most part, the style is similar to nineteenth-century British novels, relying on a third-person narrative, descriptive passages, dialogue, and the aside—a comment addressed to the reader.

The Mature Style. Beginning with *The Making of Americans*, Stein explored increasingly difficult and unique styles. The repetitious, exhaustive paragraphs of *The Making of Americans*, the spare abstract impressionism of *Tender Buttons*, and the wild experimentalism of *Four Saints in Three Acts* (1934) all stand as monuments to the experimentalism of the modern period. It was difficult to find an audience for these revolutionary texts, as they are unique and at times bizarre, yet Stein was simply expressing her forward-thinking ideology on art in her chosen field, writing.

Later Years. Stein had some success on the stage with her revolutionary operas, but her greatest success on the written page came when she was fifty-nine with the publication in 1933 of *The Autobiography of Alice B. Toklas*, a memoir of the Parisian salon era that was a great success in the United States. The book marks a change in style for Stein, who wrote it in a conversational tone without ambiguity. She termed it her "money-making" style. Although she continued to write theoretical works, her last works are about the experience of living through World War II and

print were some of her word portraits, works that examined a personality without attempting to tell a story in the traditional way.

Early Writings. Stein's letters and essays, written in college, bear her unmistakable style—her repetitions and idiosyncratic punctuation. At this point in her development, she included "optional" punctuation and words in parentheses, creating a multilayered effect in which the reader chooses whether to include a word or comma in a sentence.

are written in the easiest, most accessible style that she had yet adopted.

BIBLIOGRAPHY

Bridgman, Richard. *Gertrude Stein in Pieces*. New York: Oxford University Press, 1970.

Brinnin, John Malcolm. *The Third Rose: Gertrude Stein and Her World*. Boston: Little, Brown, 1959.

Greenfield, Howard. *Gertrude Stein: A Biography*. New York: Crown, 1973.

Hoffman, Michael J. *Critical Essays on Gertrude Stein*. Boston: G. K. Hall, 1986.

Kellner, Bruce, ed. *A Gertrude Stein Companion*. New York: Greenwood Press, 1988.

Newman, Shirley, and Ira B. Nadel, eds. *Gertrude Stein and the Making of Literature*. Boston: Northeastern University Press, 1988.

Rogers, W. G. *Gertrude Stein Is Gertrude Stein Is Gertrude Stein: Her Life and Work*. New York: Thomas J. Crowell, 1973.

Stendahl, Renate. *Gertrude Stein in Words and Pictures*. Chapel Hill, N.C.: Algonquin, 1994.

Sutherland, Donald. *Gertrude Stein: A Biography of Her Work*. New York: Crown, 1951.

SOME INSPIRATIONS BEHIND STEIN'S WORK

Gertrude Stein wrote at great length about her everyday life with Alice B. Toklas. Since Toklas was, for most of Stein's career, the first reader and critic of everything Stein wrote, she was undoubtedly an important influence on Stein's writing. Stein was fond of writing in a conversational style in which two voices appear be trading remarks, although the speakers are never identified. Some critics have argued that Toklas in fact wrote some passages credited to Stein, but convincing proof has never been provided. It is more likely that Stein was simply echoing and at times even transcribing the conversations she and Toklas had.

Although Stein spent many hours immersed in the literature of earlier eras, she remained a modernist, and Picasso, the most famous artist of that movement, was one of her greatest inspirations. Stein and Picasso met and became friends in 1905, when Picasso was an unappreciated, struggling artist. Stein bought many of his paintings and sat for portraits at a time when he could not make enough money painting to support his family. The largest proportion of the paintings that made up Stein's collection were by Picasso. Over the years she split with many of her friends, but her friendship with Picasso endured. Stein saw herself as a sort of literary counterpart to Picasso the visual artist, and in his prolific production, his individuality, and his restless style-shifting can be seen a parallel to Stein's own varied and unique career.

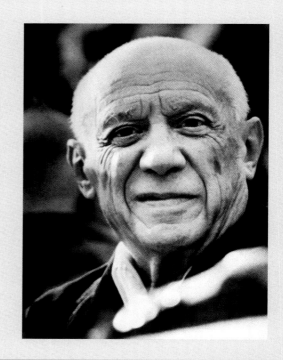

Stein and the artist Pablo Picasso, seen here in 1972, struck up a longtime friendship, and he regularly attended her famous salons.

Gertrude Stein's Salon Life

Despite the importance of Gertrude Stein's revolutionary writing style and her place as literary innovator, she is perhaps best known as the hostess of one of the most famous salons of the twentieth century. The salon, where many great painters and writers were to gather and meet, got its start when Stein's brother Leo decided to move to Paris, France, in order learn about the new movements in art. His intention was to become a painter; he moved into an apartment at 27 rue de Fleurus, on the city's bohemian Left Bank, where he planned to set up his studio.

The walls of Stein (right) and Toklas's home at 27 Rue de Fleurus were covered with the paintings of such esteemed artists as Picasso, Renoir, Gauguin, and Cezanne. Even more unhung masterpieces were stacked in corners and overflowed into every room of the house.

In 1905 Stein agreed to model for Picasso. Reflecting back on the now-famous portrait, she said, "I was and still am satisfied with my portrait, for me it is I, and it is the only reproduction of me which is always I, for me."

The Salon's Beginnings. In 1904 Stein decided to relocate and join her brother. Leo's interest in painting led the two of them to begin collecting paintings. They purchased works by established local artists as well as by those who were still struggling. Some of their first purchases included works by Eugene Delacroix and Henri de Toulouse-Lautrec as well as Paul Cézanne's *Portrait of Madame Cézanne* (1877).

Cézanne was an established member of the cubist movement in painting, a movement that had scandalized the art world with its unconventional use of shape and color. Stein later said that she got ideas for writing from looking at Cézanne's painting, the focus of which is diffuse, with different sections being weighted more or less equally in relation to the rest of the composition. Stein was later to say that at the time when she was at work on *The Making of Americans,* she "was obsessed by this idea of composition."

Stein and her brother also bought paintings by Matisse and Picasso, and Matisse became a frequent guest, admiring their collection. Soon, as Stein said, "Matisse brought people, everybody brought somebody and they came at any time and it began to be a nuisance and it was in this way that Saturday evenings began." Leo, who had been a philosophy student, led the guests in discussions of the paintings.

The Salon's Participants. Guests included Etta and Clara Cone, sisters who first accompanied Stein to Paris; her friend Mabel Dodge; and Michael and Sarah Stein, Stein's older brother and sister-in-law, who also had a home nearby. Artists included Matisse, Picasso, Marcel Duchamp, Henri Rousseau, Georges Braque, and Juan Gris; writers included the poet Guillaume Apollinaire. Stein's devoted friend Carl Van Vechten, who was to arrange for her lecture tour of the United States, was also in attendance. This group, led by expatriate Americans, became patrons of the modern art movement. In addition to buying paintings by struggling artists, these American patrons hosted the artists at their homes, feeding and encouraging them.

The outbreak of World War I in 1914 dispersed the artists and patrons of the Steins' salon. Braque and Apollinaire joined the French army. Braque was wounded in action, and Apollinaire died a few days before the war ended. Leo and Van Vechten decided to return to the United States to wait out the uncertain times. The war had disrupted the lives of the Parisians, but as they began to return to the city, the salon was revived. New friends joined the circle, and Paris again became the exciting center of artistic and literary innovation.

The Postwar Salons. In the postwar salons, Alice B. Toklas, who had moved into the residence before the war, adopted the role of hostess, entertaining the wives in the kitchen. Leo, who had always dominated the salon discussions before the war, was now living in the United States, so Stein was finally able to emerge as host. Her reputation as a writer was growing, and a new generation of writers and artists sought her out.

T. S. Eliot, Sherwood Anderson, Ernest Hemingway, William Carlos Williams, Ezra Pound, and F. Scott Fitzgerald all enjoyed Stein's friendship and support. Stein often quarreled with her new protégés, however, and many of them stopped visiting for one reason or another. Toklas, who had taken on the role of gatekeeper, became protective of Stein. When visitors who had fallen out of favor arrived at the door, Toklas informed them that they were no longer welcome. In this way, she shielded Stein from the vicissitudes of being the sought-after patron and literary sensation.

The Shifting Circle. At one point, nearly all salon attendees were banished or stopped coming of their own accord. According to Stein and Toklas, Stein's literary rival Pound, during a discussion one evening, became so excited that he fell from his chair, breaking a lamp and the chair leg. When he expressed a desire to visit them again, he was told that they were too busy picking wildflowers to receive him.

Hemingway, a twenty-three-year-old former ambulance driver, was entertained at the apartment, and soon became a favorite salon attendee. In *A Moveable Feast* (1964), he recalls arriving at the apartment for a visit and overhearing Stein and Toklas quarreling. He left and decided not to return. According to Williams's autobiography, Williams's banishment stemmed from some unflattering remarks about Stein's work: He was purportedly asked what should be done with the unpublished manuscripts; his response was that the best one should be saved and the rest thrown in the fire. He was never permitted to return.

Ernest Hemingway, seen here in March 1938, said of meeting Stein, "It was a vital day for me when I stumbled upon you." Later, when the friendship became somewhat strained, Hemingway's comments would not be so positive.

SOURCES FOR FURTHER STUDY

Hemingway, Ernest. *A Moveable Feast*. New York: Charles Scribner's Sons, 1964.

Souhani, Diana. *Gertrude and Alice*. London: HarperCollins, 1991.

Stein, Gertrude. *The Autobiography of Alice B. Toklas*. New York: The Literary Guild, 1933.

Williams, William Carlos. *The Autobiography of William Carlos Williams*. New York: Random House, 1951.

Reader's Guide to Major Works

THE AUTOBIOGRAPHY OF ALICE B. TOKLAS

Genre: Nonfiction
Subgenre: Memoir
Published: New York, 1933
Time period: 1875–1935
Setting: Paris, France; Oakland, California

Themes and Issues. Gertrude Stein's memoir of bohemian life in Paris is her most widely read book and the greatest literary success of her life. It is a witty, entertaining collection of gossip about the many personalities of the modern art world whom she befriended during her years in Paris. By the 1930s, when the book was published, many writers and artists who had struggled in anonymity were finally becoming celebrities, and the American public was hungry for anecdotes about the artists Pablo Picasso, Henri Matisse, and Georges Braque and the writer Ernest Hemingway. The book is a questionable piece of history, however, for it is first an entertainment and second a self-promotion on Stein's part. Stein was attempting to show that she was more than the remote, inaccessible theoretician of the avant-garde—the group that developed new or experimental concepts in the arts—that her earlier works represented. As such, the book is more subjective than factual.

The Plot. To create her best-seller, Stein adopted the voice of her companion, Alice B. Toklas, and she was so successful that some critics argued that Toklas had in fact written some or all of the book. Stein was, however, well known for her ability as a mimic, and *The Autobiography of Alice B. Toklas* is only one of many works that she wrote in the voice of another.

She adopted Toklas's voice in writing her own memoir for several different reasons. First, Stein and Toklas always joked that Toklas had the better memory of the pair, and it was Toklas's memory of events that became the accepted version of how things had happened. Therefore when Stein relented and began to write her memoirs, a task she had avoided but that many of her friends had long requested, she wrote Toklas's version of how things had happened in the way that Toklas had told the story. This trick of hiding behind the voice and personality of another allowed Stein to write about herself without seeming to do so. Stein's primary purpose in writing *The Autobiography*

Pavel Tchelitchew's painting *Alice B. Toklas* (National Portrait Gallery, Washington, D.C.) captures the pensive, quiet nature of Stein's lifelong partner. The *Atlantic Monthly* serialization of *The Autobiography of Alice B. Toklas* won Stein an even wider readership. Checks began pouring in, prompting the writer to quip, "I love being rich, . . . not as yet so awful rich but with prospects, it makes me all cheery inside."

of *Alice B. Toklas* was self-justification—to explain herself and her methods to her critics.

Analysis. In this book Stein shows the commonsense, down-to-earth woman, the lovable eccentric, and the "genius," all at the same time. There was no better way to show herself as she was than to show herself as seen through the eyes of Toklas, her greatest and most loyal fan. The device allows Stein to indulge in the most shameless self-promotion, instead of remaining modestly restrained.

Stein was happy with the money and celebrity that *The Autobiography of Alice B. Toklas* brought, but she worried that her personality would become more popular than her writing. In one sense, this anticipation proved to be the case, but in another, Stein's personal popularity could not have emerged until after the production of her most inaccessible and difficult writing. Her writing would not be read as widely as it is today if it were not for her charming personality and wit and for the interesting life she led.

Many of Stein's friends and acquaintances were unhappy with the way they were portrayed in her book. They felt that Stein had misrepresented her position in the early modern art culture of Paris. *The Autobiography of Alice B. Toklas* puts Stein very squarely at the center of the exciting time but does not mention her brother Leo, who in fact introduced her to collecting. Leo was very upset over this omission, and Hemingway, Pound, and Braque were displeased at their portrayals in the book. A group of artists, led by Braque, even published a challenge to the book's accuracy, "Testimony Against Gertrude Stein," in the Paris journal *Transition*. In the end such squabbles have not diminished the stature of the book as Stein's most widely read and enjoyed piece and the best and liveliest memoir of the Paris art scene in the first half of the twentieth century.

SOURCES FOR FURTHER STUDY

Hemingway, Ernest. *A Moveable Feast*. New York: Charles Scribner's Sons, 1964.

Hobhouse, Janet. *Everybody Who Was Anybody*. London: Weidenfield and Nicolson, 1975.

Mellow, James R. *Charmed Circle: Gertrude Stein and Company*. London: Phaidon Press, 1974.

Souhani, Diana. *Gertrude and Alice*. London: HarperCollins, 1991.

Toklas, Alice B. *What Is Remembered*. New York: Holt, Rinehart and Winston, 1963.

White, Ray Lewis. *Sherwood Anderson/Gertrude Stein: Correspondence and Personal Essays*. Chapel Hill: University of North Carolina Press.

THE MAKING OF AMERICANS
Genre: Novel
Subgenre: Family history
Published: Paris, 1925
Time period: 1850–1910
Setting: Baltimore, Maryland

Themes and Issues. Stein wrote *The Making of Americans* between 1902 and 1911. Her friends and visitors were the only people to see it over the next fourteen years. After being rejected in Europe and America, *The Making of Americans* was finally published in 1925. Stein's version of the epic novel is 926 pages long, and it makes for some difficult reading. The book's subjects are the somewhat fictionalized lives of Stein's extended family, but like much of Stein's writing, ideas and style overwhelm the plot.

The Plot. *The Making of Americans* starts with autobiographical descriptions of Stein's grandmothers, who immigrate to America, and the marriage of her mother and father. The story of the Hersland family, as they are called in the novel, continues with Stein's generation, with Stein being analogous to the character of Martha Hersland. The book is, however, not a typical novel, and the plot lines, characters, and style change throughout.

Stein began the book in a somewhat conventional style, but as she wrote, her ideas progressed, and the subject matter and style changed. Whereas early in the book an attempt at story is made, the later pages contain longer paragraphs and longer sentences that leave the

Stein once wrote, "When I began writing I was always writing about beginning again and again. In *The Making of Americans* I was making a continuous present a continuous beginning again and again. . . . " As in Diana Ong's 2000 painting *People, People – Plus,* the scope of Stein's work widens as it progresses, trying to take in multiple existences.

plot behind and instead investigate philosophical questions of perception, memory, and the act of communicating with a reader. *The Making of Americans* is undisciplined compared with ordinary novels, but in it Stein was more concerned with recording ideas as they came to her than with telling a conventional story.

Analysis. Although the writing does not seem clinical or analytical, Stein's background in psychology led to her desire truly to understand the real personality, or "bottom nature," of a person. It is the primary example of the repetitious style that she also utilized in the word portraits she wrote from 1905 to 1920.

The book is repetitious because Stein believed people are always repeating themselves. She believed that the key to understanding a personality was to listen to the repetitions in the person's conversation and sense the "movement" behind them. People reveal themselves slowly, and so in attempting to describe a person, the same sort of repetition and patience is required.

The book contains sentences that express the ceaseless, repetitive inner lives of the characters. Stein was well ahead of her time in attempting this sort of writing. Many of the other noted stream-of-consciousness novels, such as those by James Joyce, William Faulkner, and

Virginia Woolf, were not written until the 1920s.

The Making of Americans claims to be a book that describes every sort of person and personality in existence—or, as Stein put it, "a history of every one who ever can or is or was or will be living." However, the book is autobiographical and can be seen as Stein's attempt to understand her own personality.

Stein began writing the notebooks that became *The Making of Americans* at an unhappy time in her life, after the failure of her college relationship with May Bookstaver. Always an emotional yet analytical person, she wrote about this unhappy relationship from different perspectives in several of her early works before putting it behind her as she began her more happy relationship with Toklas. *The Making of Americans* was written at a period of great change in Stein's life during which she progressed from unsure young woman to a more serene, mature woman, and the book contains all the soul-searching that went into that transition.

SOURCES FOR FURTHER STUDY

Hoffman, Michael J. *Gertrude Stein*. Boston: Twayne Publishers, 1976.

Kawin, Bruce F. *Telling It Again and Again*. Ithaca, N.Y.: Cornell University Press, 1972.

Walker, Jayne L. *The Making of a Modernist: Gertrude Stein from "Three Lives" to "Tender Buttons."* Amherst: University of Massachusetts Press, 1984.

TENDER BUTTONS: OBJECTS, FOOD, ROOMS

Genre: Prose poem
Subgenre: Experimental
Published: New York, 1914
Time period: Eternal present
Setting: Unnamed rooms

Themes and Issues. Intensely modern and adventuresome in style, *Tender Buttons* is a unique work of literature. Stein always ranked it among her most important books because it was the first of her works to be written in the fully evolved "cubist" style, toward which she had been moving in earlier works. In cubist painting, a person or object is represented not simply from a single point of view but from many varying points of view.

Painters began to work in the cubist style because they realized that in showing an object or person from the front, other views of the object, such as from the back or top, are not seen, and the object is represented only partially. Therefore, painters such as Georges Braque, Juan Gris, and Stein's great friend Picasso began to show multiple views of their subjects integrated into single compositions on the canvas. By painting in this manner, these artists were able to move beyond simple representation, a function of painting that was being displaced by photography.

In *Tender Buttons*, Stein applied these cubist ideas to her own artistic medium, literature. In earlier works she had focused on personalities, trying to describe the psychology of her characters as deeply and as completely as possible, but in *Tender Buttons* she decided to turn her investigation to objects. She turned to "still life" representation because objects inspired less emotional reaction when she considered them than did people, and in developing this new style, she wanted to avoid emotion. The trademark repetitions of earlier works are replaced by a spare, economical style with no wasted words.

The Plot. In earlier works, Stein departed from conventional grammar and narrative, but the combinations of words that made up the sentences were still comprehensible. Even if meaning was sometimes elusive, an impression that meaning was intended remained.

In "Objects" and "Food," however, Stein moves further away from objective meaning into a new kind of writing, a new attempt at capturing the eternal present. There is therefore no standard plot, as with the work of other writers. The third section of *Tender Buttons*, "Rooms," is not divided into sections the way the previous two chapters are, but the style is similar. "No eye-glasses are rotten, no window is useless and yet if air will not come in there is

The cubist style of Pablo Picasso, exemplified in his 1932 oil painting *Still Life: Bust, Bowl and Pallette* (Musée Picasso, Paris), greatly influenced Stein's *Tender Buttons: Objects, Food, and Room* and other works. Some critics dubbed her experimental prose "literary cubism."

a speech ready, there always is and there is no dimness, not a bit of it."

Critics writing about *Tender Buttons* are for the most part divided, either dismissing it as lunatic ravings or trying to decipher it as if it were a code or puzzle. Attempts at explaining the work have met with some success, but the effort that has been put into decoding *Tender Buttons* and the other works Stein wrote in this style is somewhat misplaced. The wonder of *Tender Buttons* is that it exists in its own right; it does not attempt to tell a story or to describe to the reader the objects, food, or rooms of Stein's life. Instead, the sentences of the book relate only to themselves, to their own compositions, and the words lose their traditional meanings and associations, thereby gaining new freedom in their ability to startle and provoke.

Analysis. The short book is divided into three chapters: "Objects," "Food," and "Rooms." The first two chapters are divided into paragraphs and sentences, each with its own title. These sections do not describe in the traditional sense the objects named in their titles, as in describing a bottle as "green" or a wall as "plaster," nor do they describe the object in a metaphorical sense. In fact, they do not describe objects in any usual way. Stein contemplated an object and then recorded the associations that occurred to her. She was trying in this manner to capture the object as it existed in her mind at the moment. The results are at times abstract and difficult, as in this example: "MALACHITE. The sudden spoon is the same in no size. The sudden spoon is the wound in the decision." This sort of writing essentially defies understanding and interpretation.

SOURCES FOR FURTHER STUDY

DeKoven, Marianne. *A Different Language: Gertrude Stein's Experimental Writing.* Madison: University of Wisconsin Press, 1983.

Knapp, Bettina. *Gertrude Stein.* New York: Continuum, 1990.

Ruddick, Lisa. *Reading Gertrude Stein: Body, Text, Gnosis.* Ithaca, N.Y.: Cornell University Press, 1990.

Other Works

BREWSIE AND WILLIE (1946). Gertrude Stein's last novel, *Brewsie and Willie,* is a book comprising a series of conversations among American soldiers in Europe following the end of World War II. Stein spent a large portion of her final two years in the company of American soldiers after the liberation of France. She entertained many of the passing troops in Paris and accompanied some to Berlin, Germany, to view the remains of the Nazi headquarters after the war. *Brewsie and Willie* is written in the conversational style that Stein favored. She made use of competing voices to discuss a topic because she could, in effect, argue with herself and interject opposing points as they occurred to her.

In the novel, Brewsie represents Stein. He is the contemplative liberal of the group of soldiers. Willie, on the other hand, is tough, sarcastic, and conservative. The two characters balance each other in a series of debates about life in the United States. The central idea that emerges from these debates is that the comfortable life of the average American comes at the expense of individualism. The Industrial Revolution and the impact it had on American culture seem to be Stein's main targets, the greed of the capitalist system her main enemy. However, in letters following the publication of the book, she stated that neither communism nor socialism was the answer for the United States and that she could offer only individualism as a counterweight to the dehumanizing effects of the industrial society.

EVERYBODY'S AUTOBIOGRAPHY (1937). Stein's *Everybody's Autobiography* was written after the success of *The Autobiography of Alice B.*

Brewsie and Willie was an attempt to diagnose the somewhat troubling course Stein thought her homeland was assuming. Diego Rivera's *La Cena Capitalista* (Capitalist Dinner), which hangs in Secretaria de Educacion Publica, Mexico City, Mexico, takes a similar swipe at capitalist indulgence and excess.

problems of identity were universal concerns shared by all people.

MRS. REYNOLDS AND FIVE EARLIER NOVELETTES, 1931–1942

(1952). *Mrs. Reynolds*, the title piece of this collection, is the first of two books written while Stein was living in Belignin, France, during World War II, the other being the autobiographical diary *Wars I Have Seen*. The title character, Mrs. Reynolds, is a typical married woman in an unnamed town. She and her husband go through the routines of their daily lives as the book progresses, but the ominous cloud of war hangs over the town.

The enemy is led by Angel Harper, a shadowy figure known to the people of the town. Although Harper, who represents the German chancellor Adolf Hitler, never appears in person, his ominous rise to power is discussed by the people of the town throughout the book. Another character, Joseph Lane, is featured early in the book and is meant to represent Joseph Stalin, but his character fades as Stein concentrates on Harper. The book is written in a somewhat more difficult style than *The Autobiography of Alice B. Toklas* and *Ida: A Novel* (1941). Nevertheless, *Mrs. Reynolds* remains an effective, chilling evocation of life in the provinces of a country at war.

Toklas and is a response to that book. The latter book was written in Stein's plain-talking, or "money-making," style; *Everybody's Autobiography* is written in the Stein essay form, that is, without as much wit and with considerably more analysis and soul-searching.

After the success of *The Autobiography of Alice B. Toklas*, Stein found herself uncomfortable with the act of writing. She was aware for the first time of an audience waiting expectantly for her work, and after thirty-five years of ceaseless productivity, she found herself blocked. *Everybody's Autobiography* is the story of her becoming rich and famous and of the writer's block that followed. It is primarily concerned with identity, the identity in which Stein found herself less secure in the wake of her celebrity. The book is "everybody's" autobiography because Stein believed that these

THREE LIVES (1909). Stein paid for the initial publication of *Three Lives* herself. The first of her novels to be published, it is one of her most readable books. It has three sections chronicling the lives of three different women in Baltimore: "The Good Anna," "The Gentle Lena," and "Melanctha." Anna is an older, sharp-tongued woman who runs her household strictly. She gets good work out of her staff but only at the expense of frequent headaches. She dies still lecturing her staff on their duties. The piece is a character study, carefully observed and written in a voice that captures the German immigrant community in which Anna works.

"Melanctha" is an African American woman who works as a substitute teacher. She is a romantic, thoughtful, serious person who is romantically involved with a doctor named Jeff Campbell. Campbell is unimaginative, unfeeling, and conventional, and the tension between them leads to the doctor abandoning Melanctha, who then sickens and dies.

"The Gentle Lena" is a passive, kind woman who is manipulated into marrying by her aunt. After the marriage, Lena becomes pregnant, but both she and the child die during the delivery. Stein drew on material she gathered from her medical student work delivering babies in the poorer sections of Baltimore for this portrait, one of her most successful conventional pieces of fiction.

Resources

The major collection of Gertrude Stein's manuscripts, including letters and other personal writings, can be found in the Collection of American Literature, Beinecke Rare Book and Manuscript Library, Yale University. Other resources include the following:

Gertrude Stein's *The Autobiography of Alice B. Toklas*. This site on the World Wide Web includes background for the autobiography, complete with biographical details on some key salon attendees. Artists' biographies are accompanied by samples of their work (http://www.cwrl.utexas.edu/~natasha/usauto_html/stein/)

Gertrude Stein: *When This You See, Remember Me*. This 1970 documentary film on the writer's life was directed by Perry Miller.

***Tender Buttons*: Gertrude Stein On Line.** This Web site's mission is to "make a contribution to the worldwide appreciation of Gertrude Stein and to foster the study and performance of her work." It includes links to *Time-Sense*, an electronic quarterly on Stein's art, and a virtual salon, as well as an abstracted text of a Modern Language Association panel on Stein. (http://www.tenderbuttons.com)

JACK AKERS AND MELANIE WATKINS

Index

Page numbers in **boldface** type indicate article titles. Page numbers in *italic* type indicate illustrations.